Love Letters From God

MARIANNE VANWINGERDEN

Love Letters From God

©2022 Marianne VanWingerden

print ISBN: 978-1-66783-728-4
ebook ISBN: 978-1-66783-729-1

DEDICATION,

I dedicate this book to my Heavenly Father God and Savior Jesus Christ. It is my complete desire to honor our Lord God. Obviously this was written by human hands. But I have based the letters on the word of God and what He wants to teach us through it. Only His word alone is without flaw.

God put a dream on my heart years ago to write some of the beautiful truths of how He feels about us or what He has to teach us, from His word, into letter form. It is my desire that each individual see and feel how personal this God is that we serve.

Several years ago I was on my way home from a ladies trip to Honduras. I was thinking about "The Home" for girls, our mission, Honduras Fountain of Life (Fuenta de Vida) has there for orphan and abused girls. My heart was sad for what they have been through. God gave me the idea for an art project for them to illustrate how God sees them. A wooden box starts out scraped, scarred, burned and neglected. Then it is painted, glued with beautiful stones to form a geode and filled with tiny treasures. It struck me how much they needed to be assured that they are loved and treasured by their heavenly Father. The most important thing they need to know and that their box (signifying their body) must include was letters from a caring God. I felt strongly impressed upon that these precious wounded girls must know that their God cared deeply about what had happened to them. He knows everything. He cares. He is just and loves them (and us) immensely.

He wants to teach us. He wants us to learn, and He wants us to know the truth about how He sees us.

That art project was accomplished in February 2020. Along with the boxes, we brought a small booklet of letters that a friend and I had printed. It was my desire (or dream) that someday I would write a long version in a devotional type format.

As women we live in a broken and sinful world with broken and sinful people. (Which we all are!) We have been wronged, we are insecure, lonely, angry, fearful, jealous, and scarred. We need to know, feel and experience the truth from God's word and make it personal. He is our Lord God, our Healer and Supplier, our Master and our Sanctifier. But we can also call him our King, our Savior, our Lord and our God. This is so personal that the Master and Creator of all the universe loves us, pursues us, calls us His children and His friends! And in fact, we can call him, Abba (Daddy) Father!

This truth is so beautiful that it is hard to comprehend. That is why I wrote the letters as I did, in a personal format to speak to the women that we are and the little girls that live inside each of us. I pray that God's love and truth will reach into your hearts and bring about your healing.

Special thanks to my son Jeff who helped in all areas technical, correcting and printing.

Soli Deo Gloria

To God alone be the glory.

In His love,

Just one woman that loves His word.

Marianne

Note: I specifically wrote these letters for God's children, those that believe that God sent His Son, His only Son, perfect and holy, sent from heaven above to live on this sin covered earth. Jesus was born of a virgin, lived and died on this earth, sinless, but he took our sins upon himself and paid the price for them. He arose on the third day.

If you do not know him but have come upon this book, I pray that you would believe this in your heart too and confess this with your mouth, and then you will truly be a child of God! Every promise in His word is truth and is for you and when you die you will instantly be in heaven with your God and Savior. Together. Forever. If you do not know Him I cannot encourage you enough to seek Him in his powerful word and invite Him into your heart as Lord and Savior of your life.

PS

If a husband, brother, friend, etc. happens to pick this book up, all the words and promises are true for you too! Substitute: My son or child where appropriate.

Please check out www.HondurasFountainOfLife.org

DEAR BEAUTIFUL GIRL,

Hello My beautiful girl! My beautiful daughter! This is your Heaven Father. I want you to know how I see you. When I gaze upon you My girl, I see amazing beauty, inside and out. When I formed you in your mother's womb, I made you exactly how I wanted to make you. She will have these shapes eyes and I know exactly how tall she will grow, what her smile will look like, how her mind and heart will work. I even know the number of hairs upon your head! And when I look upon you My beautiful daughter, I see perfection. I see exquisite beauty. The world may tell you that "this" or "that" should be different with your face or body or taunt you with many lies. I am telling you that I don't make mistakes and I made you perfectly. Rejoice in that truth, that beauty, My girl. And believe it! Look to Me for the truth about you!

I love you My beautiful girl!

God

> You made all the delicate, inner parts of my body and knit me together in my mother's womb. Thank you for making me so wonderfully complex! Your workmanship is marvelous—how well I know it. You watched me as I was being formed in utter seclusion, as I was woven together in the dark of the womb. You saw me before I was born. Every day of my life was recorded in your book. Every moment was laid out before a single day had passed. How precious are your thoughts about me, O God.

5

They cannot be numbered! I can't even count them; they outnumber the grains of sand! And when I wake up, you are still with me! Psalm 139: 13-18 NLT

You are altogether beautiful, my darling, beautiful in every way. Song of Solomon 4:7 NLT

DEAR PRAYING GIRL,

Come to Me often, My daughter and talk with Me. You need My help. You need Me to listen. You need someone to pour your heart out to and that is Me. It is never too much for Me and there is no limit to how much or how often you can speak to Me! I love to hear from you and I want to give you a solution to your problems. Why would you carry a burden on your own? I know you are tired. I know you are hurting and overwhelmed. Bring your troubles to Me, My child. There is nothing too small or too large to bring to Me. I am always here for you. I am the same God yesterday, today, and forever. I am still in the business of miracles. My timing and My ways of how I answer will not be as you may choose, but there's always a reason for each of My answers, and I will choose whatever is best for you. You can rest in that truth even if you don't understand it. My precious love, pray with faith, pray without ceasing, and give thanks in every circumstance for this is My will for you in My beloved Son Christ Jesus.

Love from,

Your Listening God.

> Rejoice always, pray without ceasing, give thanks in all circumstances; for this is the will of God in Christ Jesus for you. 1 Thessalonians 5:16-18 ASV

And pray in the Spirit on all occasions with all kinds of prayers and requests. With this in mind, be alert and always keep on praying for all the Lord's people. Ephesians 6:18 NIV

DEAR LOVED GIRL,

You are so very loved My daughter. Do you know that? My love is everlasting and unfailing. My love is gracious and compassionate and it endures forever! My love is eternal. Every person on this earth at one time or another will disappoint you, let you down, or break your heart. People are mean, cruel, abusive, untrue, unfaithful, unkind and fickle. They remove their love. But I will never do that. My love is for always and forever. This means that you can trust Me in any and every situation because what I choose for you is chosen through a filter of great love. I love you, yes you, My daughter, so much that I sent My Son, My only Son, My sinless Son to come and pay the price for your sins so that you could be with Me forever. That is unfathomable and immeasurable love. I gave you life. I gave you love. I gave you grace. I gave you mercy. I gave you My Son. And I continue to give you all of these things. I do not withdraw My love. Ever. Never. It is for always and forever and one day when it is time for you to come to Me, we will be together forever! Think on these things My beloved daughter. Feel loved, so very loved, so very loved by Me. You have a beautiful hopeful future, and will be with Me forever. Eternal and agape love from your everlasting Father, forever and forever and ever...

God

> "I have loved you with an everlasting love; I have drawn
> you with unfailing kindness. Jeremiah 31:3 NIV

But from everlasting to everlasting the LORD's love is with those who fear him, and his righteousness with their children's children. Psalm 103:17 NIV

For the LORD is good, and His loving devotion endures forever; His faithfulness continues to all generations. Psalm 100:5 BSB

Give thanks to the LORD, for he is good! His faithful love endures forever. Give thanks to the God of gods. His faithful love endures forever. Give thanks to the Lord of lords. His faithful love endures forever. Psalm 136:1-3 NLT

DEAR WEEPING GIRL,

I have seen you my daughter, I have heard you. Nothing is hidden from Me and nothing is a surprise to Me. What I want you to know though is how much your tears mean to Me. They represent your pain and your pain and everything about you matters so deeply to Me. I have designed tears to actually be healing when they are released from your body. Did you know that? Emotional tears release stress hormones and natural pain killers. They are different then other types of tears. There is a type of protein in them that is in a tear of pain and not at times that your eyes are watering because of something else. I have truly thought of everything. Back to how much your tears mean to Me. Did you know that I keep all the tears that you have shed in a bottle? It's hard for you to fathom isn't it? But it's true and My word confirms it. Not only that, but I have recorded each and every tear in My book. My precious daughter, never forget what your tears mean to Me! I want to dry those tears My darling. I will wipe everyone of them away. I will exchange your sorrows for joy, your mourning for dancing and one day, My love, you will have everlasting joy with Me in heaven forever-where no tear will ever be shed again!

Love from your Abba,

God

> ...Weeping may last through the night, but joy comes with the morning. Psalm 30:5b NLT

You have turned my mourning into joyful dancing. You have taken away my clothes of mourning and clothed me with joy... Psalm 30:11 NLT

You keep track of all my sorrows. You have collected all my tears in your bottle. You have recorded each one in your book. Psalm 56:8 NLT

DEAR HOPEFUL GIRL,

Hope is such a beautiful thing! I want you to be filled with it My daughter. You must have hope to live and move forward and I have a bible full of hope and promises for you. I am the God of hope! If you choose My hope, you can be filled with joy and peace because you trust in Me. Then you will overflow with confident hope through the power of the Holy Spirit. Isn't that the way you want to live each day? Living in hope, and trust, and joy, and peace, and love, in My promises? What a beautiful place that is to live! And when something overflows, what happens? It pours onto something or someone else. I want you to be so filled with My word and the Holy Spirit that you just overflow with hope, joy, love, peace and trust. Others will see that you are different and want what you have and you will be My witness. Be ready to explain why you have such hope and Who your hope is in! Live this way as you await the blessed hope and glorious appearance of your great God and Savior Jesus Christ. Live in joyful and faithful expectation: Hope. So much love My daughter.

From,

Your God of Hope.

> Such hope never disappoints or deludes us, for God's love
> has been poured out in our hearts through the Holy Spirit
> Who has been given to us. Romans 5:5 AMPC

I wait for the Lord, I expectantly wait, and in His word do I hope. Psalm 130:5 AMPC

But those who hope in the LORD will renew their strength. They will soar on wings like eagles; they will run and not grow weary, they will walk and not be faint. Isaiah 40:31 NIV

DEAR WOUNDED GIRL,

It hurts Me to write those words, My precious wounded daughter. How dare another human being hurt, wound, abuse, scar, belittle or harm My precious daughter in any way, shape or form! You cannot imagine or even fathom the boiling rage this causes Me! I HATE sin with an everlasting hatred. I HATE and despise wrong and evil done to My little daughter. Please realize that there will be justice for you! I promise that My girl. My word promises that! If someone sows evil, they will reap evil. I am your advocate, your lawyer, and your judge. Vengeance is Mine and I will repay! Rest in that My girl. Rest in the fact that I am working for you. Let Me heal you. Give Me your wounds, your heart, your ashes and I will give you beauty instead! Open up your heart to all I have for you. It is beautiful beyond your wildest imagination. I love you, My dear wounded girl. But soon, I will be able to call you My healed girl…

Much love,

from your Father, your Lawyer, your Advocate, and the Judge working for you!

> To grant [consolation and joy] to those who mourn in Zion—to give them an ornament (a garland or diadem) of beauty instead of ashes, the oil of joy instead of mourning, the garment [expressive] of praise instead of a heavy, burdened, and failing spirit—that they may be called oaks of righteousness [lofty, strong, and magnificent, distinguished for uprightness, justice, and right standing with God], the planting of the Lord, that He may be glorified. Isaiah 61:3 AMPC

> Lord, You have pleaded the causes of my soul [You have managed my affairs and You have protected my person and my rights]; You have rescued and redeemed my life! O Lord, You have seen my wrong [done to me]; judge and maintain my cause. You have seen all their vengeance, all their devices against me. Lamentations 3:58-60 AMPC

> He heals the broken hearted and binds up their wounds. Psalm 147:3 NIV

DEAR KIND GIRL,

Hello my kind girl! My kind daughter! I put kindness into your heart. Use it. When I made this earth, this world, I made it in utter perfection. Every aspect that you can imagine, and all that you cannot, were made absolutely perfectly. But I did allow choice to this human race I created. And when the evil one, and sin and selfishness and wrong choices are made, my children are hurt. First of all, I am asking that you would not blame Me for the sin of human beings. I cannot even look upon darkness, and I would never and cannot do evil. No, humans on this earth have chosen to hurt you, My daughter. I have many things to write to you and I will explain some of the things that you are confused about. But know that there are definitely times in this life when you will not know some of the answers. You will not know how all the pieces of your life fit together and what I have done on your behalf until you are in heaven. But know this My child: You can trust Me. I am the God of Justice. For right now, My purpose is to remind you to be kind. Do not repay evil for evil. Do not be unkind to others because of the hurts and injustices that you have suffered. Give back goodness and kindness to everyone you encounter. You may believe that you are incapable of this and I will tell you that you are right! But with My help, you can do anything! My well never runs dry so I can continually refill you with kindness.

I love you, My kind daughter.

God.

17

Do not become overcome by evil, but overcome evil with good. Romans 12:21 NIV

Never return evil for evil or insult for insult (scolding, tongue-lashing, berating), but on the contrary blessing [praying for their welfare, happiness, and protection, and truly pitying and loving them]. For know that to this you have been called, that you may yourselves inherit a blessing [from God—that you may obtain a blessing as heirs, bringing welfare and happiness and protection]. 1 Peter 3:9 AMPC

And become useful and helpful and kind to one another, tenderhearted (compassionate, understanding, loving-hearted), forgiving one another [readily and freely], as God in Christ forgave you. Ephesians 4:32 AMPC

DEAR GRATEFUL GIRL OF MINE,

Remember to always give thanks My child. I give you many, many blessings every day. It is important to keep your eyes open, pay attention and then acknowledge the blessings I have given you by thanking Me. It is a discipline but also a joy. It will bring you joy to notice and thank Me many times a day. Not only does this make you think of Me, it keeps you searching for My goodness to you, My blessings. This is possible even in hardships, trials and pain. When you are actively searching for My blessings you are searching for Me and how much I love you. You can find Me in every natural thing I have made and you will be astounded by what I have created. Do you know that I could have made the whole world in shades of black, white and gray? But look at the vibrant colors I have given you in the sky, clouds, trees and flowers, fruit and everything and everyone you see around you! This is a blessing! What about the different types and flavorful foods you eat? I didn't give you manna alone but gladly have given you food to delight your tongue and senses. More blessings! What about a baby's laugh, it's soft skin and luminous eyes? Do you have a bed to sleep in? Clothes on your back? A friend, a husband, parents, a child or a co-worker you can talk to? And so on and on it goes My daughter. Look for the blessings, even in hardships. They drive you to Me, to your knees in prayer and to My word. In all things give thanks for this is God's will for you in Christ Jesus. Give thanks with a grateful heart My Girl and remember that every perfect gift comes from above, from the Father of lights, from the Lord of love. That father is your Father and I am telling you this to gently lead you to something you need to do for your own good and to honor your Heavenly Father. I love you and I am looking forward to hearing from you. Make it daily my girl!

Your Heavenly Father,
The gift Giver and Lord of lights.

> Every good gift and every perfect (free, large, full) gift is from above; it comes down from the Father of all [that gives] light, in [the shining of] Whom there can be no variation [rising or setting] or shadow cast by His turning [as in an eclipse]. James 1:17 AMPC

> Thank [God] in everything [no matter what the circumstances may be, be thankful and give thanks], for this is the will of God for you [who are] in Christ Jesus [the Revealer and Mediator.] 1 Thessalonians 5:8 AMPC

> This is the day that the LORD has made; let us rejoice and be glad in it. Psalm 118:24 HCSB

> To the end that my tongue and my heart and everything glorious within me may sing praise to You and not be silent. Oh Lord my God, I will give thanks to you forever. Psalm 30:12 AMP

DEAR FORGIVING GIRL,

It's a lot to ask, I know that. I know that your body was used and abused. Your mind is scarred and your heart is full of anger and rage. I understand. I always understand. I am asking you to forgive for your own good. You are worried that if you forgive those that have so horribly wronged you, it's like saying that it was OK. No it was not! Not in any way, shape, or form! You are afraid that if you let go of your anger that you will set that person free. That somehow if you let go of your rage, that person is not responsible anymore for what they have done to you. That is not true at all My child. They are responsible and I will handle them. Trust Me and let My vengeance do it's work. I ask you to forgive to set YOU free! It is for your good My girl, for your healing. Open your heart and hands and give Me that great weight. Let go and I will carry it for you. Let the healing begin My forgiving daughter.

So much love from you Fearsome and Fierce Father,

> For we know Him who said, " Vengeance is Mine [retribution and the deliverance of justice rest with Me], I will repay [the wrongdoer]." And again, " The Lord will judge His people." Hebrews 10:30 AMP

> For if you forgive others their trespasses [their reckless and willful sins], your heavenly Father will also forgive you. Matthew 6:14 AMP

Lord, you are my lawyer! Plead my case! For you have redeemed my life. You have seen the wrong they have done to me, LORD . Be my judge, and prove me right. You have seen the vengeful plots my enemies have laid against me. LORD, you have heard the vile names they call me. You know all about the plans they have made. My enemies whisper and mutter as they plot against me all day long. Look at them! Whether they sit or stand, I am the object of their mocking songs. Pay them back, LORD, for all the evil they have done. Lamentations 3:58-64 NLT

DEAR COMPLETE GIRL,

My dear daughter, seek completeness in Me. Each human being has an emptiness, a God – shaped need within them. This need can never be filled by another person or thing. You cannot be fulfilled by a boyfriend, a husband, a child, or a family of your own. A higher education, a car, a house, or a great job, cannot fill you up or meet the need in your heart. Food, alcohol, things, fame or people's approval cannot and will not meet your needs, because they are not your needs. I am your need. I can fill your life, your heart, your need with love and joy and peace and rest. There is only one thing that can complete you in this life and it is Me. Turn to Me for everything, and every need My daughter. Believe in My Precious Son and all that he did for you and then you will truly be complete.

So much love,

From your Heavenly Father.

> For in Christ lives all the fullness of God in a human body. So you also are complete through your union with Christ, who is the ruler over every ruler and authority.
> Colossians 2:9-10 NLT

DEAR TREASURED GIRL!

My dear daughter, do you know that you are My treasure? Yes, it's true! You are My special treasure, My treasured possession and My jewel. As in treasured possession, I mean the most special and valued to me, someone I want to guard and keep safe. Think of something that is your favorite, special or most valuable to you. Do you take special care of it, guard it and keep it in a safe place? That is how I think of and love you, only so much more! To be called the treasure, My treasure, My treasured possession, My jewel, by the Most High God is an honor indeed! Remember that, think about it, lock that sweetness into your mind and heart to take out and be amazed when times are hard. When you feel lonely or insecure, when others are unkind or devalue you, or ugly memories come to your mind, choose that time to remember how I treasure you, how I value you, and that you are My jewel and favored one! I love you My dearest one.

God

> And they shall be Mine, says the LORD of hosts, on that day that I make them My jewels (My special treasure, My peculiar possession). And I will spare them as a man spares his own son who serves him. Malachi 3:17 AMPC

> You will also be [considered] a crown of glory and splendor in the hand of the LORD, And a royal diadem [exceedingly beautiful] in the hand of your God. Isaiah 62:3 AMP

DEAR BRAVE GIRL,

Healing from past wounds is a very difficult thing to do and it takes great bravery. Why? Because digging up these memories to lay them before Me and ask Me to heal them is not easy. To write down the wrongs or ask for help is scary. To actually make these words of terrible wrongs perpetrated against you come out of your mouth so another person can hear them and help you is like chewing on glass. No one really knows what you have been through but another person who has been through the exact same thing. And Me. I know and I care. The evil one loves lies and secrets. He want you to think that you will never be healed and that you should be ashamed. But he is a liar, remember? A secret exposed loses its power! And more importantly than that, there is something else that you need to remember: I am the Great Physician! I am your Healer! I sent My Son to bind up your wounds. By his stripes you are healed! You are so brave My child, My daughter. Take the necessary steps to get healthy. Remember to pour out your heart to Me and I promise to hear you and listen.

Love from,

Your personal Physician

> But He was wounded for our transgressions, He was crushed for our wickedness [our sin, our injustice, our wrongdoing]; The punishment [required] for our well-being fell on Him, And by His stripes (wounds) we are healed. Isaiah 53:5 AMP

He himself bore our sins in his body on the tree, that we might die to sin and live to righteousness. By his wounds you have been healed. 1 Peter 2:24 ESV

"But I will restore you to health and heal your wounds", declares the LORD... Jeremiah 30:17 NIV

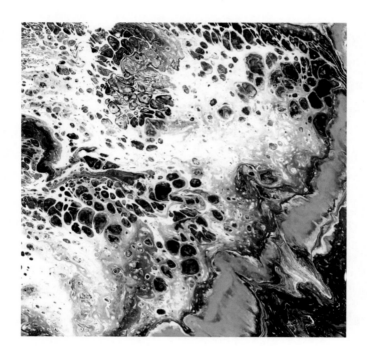

DEAR VALUABLE GIRL,

Do not believe what others say about you. People can be so harsh, mean, selfish, vindictive and jealous. They will lie to you. I want you to know the truth. You are valuable because I am telling you that you are valuable! You are valuable because I made you. In fact you are so valuable that I made you in My Own image! You are not a mistake, but a purposefully planned and made woman. I was there when you were formed in the secret place, I chose your eye color and hair color, your exact smile and the sound of your laugh. I made you on purpose and I have a purpose for your life. You are My chosen child. My fearfully and wonderfully made child. You are precious and honored in my sight. I rejoice over you with gladness and I sing loudly over you! Did you know that you are My masterpiece? Out of everything I have made, YOU are what I am most proud of. You, My precious, valuable, much loved daughter! If you ever doubt My love for you, think about this: I gave My own Son to rescue you, save you and die for you! You are absolutely priceless! Think on these things My daughter.

So much love,

from your Heavenly Father.

> The LORD your God is with you, the Mighty Warrior who saves. He will take great delight in you; in his love he will no longer rebuke you, but will rejoice over you with singing." Zephaniah 3:17 NIV

Thank you for making me so wonderfully complex!
Your workmanship is marvelous—how well I know it.
Psalm 139:14 NLT

DEAR SINGING GIRL!

Lift your praises to Me, My child! Lift your voice in joyful song. Your voice does not have to be perfect, and you don't have to know the exact words. Just open your mouth and make a joyful noise! (and If you are in a place where you can lift your arms in praise, do that also). You will not believe the difference this will make you feel physically, spiritually and emotionally. You cannot be sad when you are praising. Even if you start out in sadness, but you have made the effort to make this song come out of your mouth, you will feel a change. Sometimes praise is a sacrifice but you do it to honor Me and you will be blessed for it! And of course I always know what is best for you!

I have made singing to induce many parts of your brain simultaneously. Singing effects some of your hormones, helps alleviate stress and boosts your immune system. It can reduce pain and help with grief and improve some aspects of you physically, including increasing oxygen and strengthening the muscles involved with your lungs.

That's how it is in My earthly kingdom. Follow what I ask you to do. It is always for your protection and for your own good. And singing is one of My blessings! Lift your voice to Me in loud praise and you will feel the joy that floods your soul as you are praising Me. It is the right thing to do and while you are doing it, you also reap the benefits! Sing praises to your King!

Love,

From your Everlasting King.

Make a joyful noise unto the LORD, all the earth: make a loud noise, and rejoice, and sing praise. Psalm 98:4 KJV

Praise the LORD. How good it is to sing praises to our God, how pleasant and fitting to praise him! Psalm 147:1 NIV

Oh come, let us sing to the Lord; let us make a joyful noise to the rock of our salvation! Let us come into his presence with thanksgiving; let us make a joyful noise to him with songs of praise! Psalm 95: 1-2 ESV

DEAR WISE GIRL,

It is important to Me that you are wise. Not wise in your own eyes but with the wisdom that comes from My word and the wisdom from above. It is so worthy, so valuable and it will serve you every day of your life. Do not go with the wisdom of this world. It is very often a complete lie. The wisdom of this world is: people pleasing, proud, greedy and selfish. My wisdom is peaceful, loving and selfless. It puts Me first and then loves and serves others. My word is a feast for you! Be nourished with it every day. Seek out My will and My way. Search for My Wisdom on each and every page, every verse, each book and chapter. It will never become old because My Spirit makes it fresh each time you read it. Ask for My wisdom and I will give it to you. And each time you open My word, ask the Holy Spirit to reveal My truth to you. The wisdom, truth and love you find there will fill your heart to overflowing. Lastly My child, walk with the wise and become wise. Choose your friends and companions carefully. A wise friend will challenge you and help you to become wiser. A foolish friend will only lead you into trouble.

Much love from your,

Infinitely Wise Father.

> Do not be wise in your own eyes; Fear the Lord and shun evil. Proverbs 3:7 NIV

But the wisdom from above is first of all pure. It is also peace loving, gentle at all times, and willing to yield to others. It is full of mercy and the fruit of good deeds. It shows no favoritism and is always sincere. James 3:17 NLT

Walk with the wise and become wise; associate with fools and get in trouble. Proverbs 13:20 NLT

If you need wisdom, ask our generous God, and he will give it to you. He will not rebuke you for asking. James 1:5 NLT

DEAR HEALING GIRL,

Healing is a lot of work! It is by no means easy and does not happen without great effort. It also does not happen, and I realize that this is the part that scares you the most; but it does not happen without pain. There are many types of emotional wounds but let's compare it now to a physical wound: A physical wound can be fresh, partly healed over, gaping open, or with great infection. Also, just because there's a scar on the outside, does not mean that there is complete healing on the inside. Sometimes wounds heal on the surface and you think you are healed, or pretend that you are. But on the inside there is infection and oozing and it must come to the surface in order to be cleaned and actually healed. If that happened in a physical wound, there would need to be an operation. The doctor would need to open it up, clean all that infection out, sterilize it and then sew it up again. That's when the actual healing could begin and the wound be on it's way to being cured. So it is with emotional wounds. Sometimes you just cover things up in a temporary manner because you have so many responsibilities and such a busy life, or because you fear the whole process. You may think it's easier and less messy that way but in the long run it's actually much harder. Sometimes it's because of shame and you think it's just too painful to address. Or you are pretending that you are already healed. But on the inside the infection rages...And where there is infection, there is great pain! Yes, I know it hurts so much to have that opened up again, for that wound to be cut open and scraped out and washed clean is just excruciating. But as with any part of the physical body, when there is infection and it is not dealt with, it will infect the entire body. Ultimately, untreated, it causes death. It is your adversary, the evil one who does not want you to heal. He wants you to be miserable, bound up, imprisoned and in pain. He wants to destroy you, that's his MO, but I want you to be healed and free and fruitful for My kingdom. I know it is scary to have to go through that operation My girl, to bring things to the light, and to be scraped clean. Sometimes (usually), that takes a very long time because it is like an onion that has many layers that need to be peeled away, layer by layer, issue by issue, wound by wound. But when it's done My girl, then the healing and freedom can truly begin. And you will be healthy! You can live your life in great joy and can be an amazing help to others! Do the painful work. It is so worth it! Meanwhile and always, I AM your great Physician! I want you to be healthy in body, mind, soul and spirit. There IS healing in My Son Jesus! I'm proud of you My girl and I am always here to help you.

So much love,

From your Compassionate Father and Great Physician.

> But for you who revere my name, the sun of righteousness will rise with healing in its rays. And you will go out and frolic like well-fed calves. Malachi 4:2 NIV

> Pleasant words are like a honeycomb, Sweet and delightful to the soul and healing to the body. Proverbs 16:24 AMP

And the people all tried to touch him, because healing power went out from him, and he healed everyone. Luke 6:19 NIV

Behold, I will bring it to health and healing, and I will heal them and reveal to them abundance of prosperity and security. Jeremiah 33:6 ESV

DEAR MERCIFUL GIRL,

Isn't it a blessing that My mercies are new every morning? Think about it My girl. Each and every morning of your life is greeted with fresh mercy! My fresh mercy. And like a new day is unmarred by any wrong, so it is with My mercy. Like a stunning sunrise, colors flooding across the sky, light bursting through the trees, across mountains, over water, or wherever you are. Can you picture that beauty My girl? I know you have seen it before, probably many, many times and in several different places. I want you to think of that light bursting fourth and flooding that darkness with beauty and illumination. And then think of My mercy, coming like that •every•single•day: bright, beautiful, new, complete, lavish, fresh, loving, forgiving, endless, and such a gift! Now take that mercy that I've given to you, that I give you anew each and every day and extend it to others. My love shows through you when you extend my mercy to others. They often don't deserve it. They may have been rude to you, mean, cruel, unjust… But do you always deserve it My girl? I say that gently, just to make you think and examine your own heart, but always said in love so you will grow and live My word. I lovingly gift you with My new, fresh, daily, beautiful and endless mercy. I love you My merciful girl!

From your,

Very Merciful God.

The faithful love of the LORD never ends! His mercies never cease. Great is his faithfulness; his mercies begin afresh each morning. Lamentations 3:22-23 NLT

Blessed are the merciful, for they will be shown mercy. Matthew 5:7 NIV

Be merciful, just as your Father is merciful. Luke 6:36 NIV

mer•cy
Noun – Compassion or forgiveness show toward someone whom it is within one's power to punish or harm. (Oxford Languages)

DEAR SOWING GIRL,

My dear daughter, are you a sowing girl? What kinds of seeds are you sowing in your life? Good seeds or bad seeds? Don't be misled- you can not mock the justice of God. You will always harvest what you plant. (Galatians 6:7 NLT) How about what you are sowing in the lives of others? Are you preparing the soil, planting seeds, watering the garden or bringing in the produce? I'm not asking you to do it all. As with all things, I give certain gifts and/or responsibilities and purposes to different people. But everyone has the opportunity in their life to be sowing. You don't have to be a pastor or a missionary to sow, this is for every Christian. Day in, day out... Whose lives are you touching or who do you have the opportunity to see and show My Jesus? Actions, attitudes, integrity, your walk with Me, and the fruit of the Spirit in your life, are all opportunities for sowing. Don't forget that sometimes you will sow in tears and sometimes with joy, but it will be worth it all My dear girl! Do ask Me for wisdom and strength each time and that I would open the eyes and ears of the listener. I do My part, and I have given you tasks to do to fulfill yours. So go sow my girl! The laborers are few! Tell others about your Jesus and what he has done in your life. Tell them of his life and saving blood! If you don't tell, how will they hear? I love you My sowing girl!

Love,

From your Saving God.
And He Who first planted a garden.

Remember this: Whoever sows sparingly will also reap sparingly, and whoever sows generously will also reap generously. 2 Corinthians 9:6 NIV

These were his instructions to them: "The harvest is great, but the workers are few. So pray to the Lord who is in charge of the harvest; ask him to send more workers into his fields". Luke 10:2 NLT

Those who sow with tears will reap with songs of joy. Those who go out weeping, carrying seed to sow, will return with songs of joy, carrying sheaves with them. Psalm 126:5-6 NIV

DEAR RESTFUL GIRL,

Are you tired My daughter? Are you weary of fighting with your own heart and mind and with others? Sometimes it feels like you are fighting against the whole world, doesn't it? And you have thought about giving up before, haven't you? You can tell me, I already know all about it. I would never tell you to do that My girl. I have plans for your success. The evil one lies to you and wants your harm. Don't listen to his lies! Come to Me, My child when you are weary and burdened and I will give you rest. Take My yoke upon you and learn from me, for I am gentle and humble in heart and you will find rest for your soul. Have you ever wondered about Psalm 23 and why I have to make you rest? Because my little lamb, you would not do it on your own. You would keep pushing yourself and rushing and worrying and hurrying when what you need is rest. Humans would not stop if I had not designed the body to need sleep or if there was only daylight for 24 hours instead of having the night also. I gave you the example of rest when I designed the Sabbath. Yes I designed work, but not without rest. Follow My example My child. If you are living your life's purpose, the very plan I have for you, then what is the rush? Come away with Me, My daughter, My precious little lamb. Spend time with Me and I will refresh your soul! Come to Me and I will give you rest. Let Me carry you in my arms My little daughter.

So much love from,

Your Shepherd

Yes, my soul, find rest in God; my hope comes from him. Psalm 62:5 NIV

He makes me lie down in [fresh, tender] green pastures; he leads me beside the still and restful waters. Psalm 23:2 AMPC

Come to me, all you who are weary and burdened, and I will give you rest. Take my yoke upon you and learn from me, for I am gentle and humble in heart, and you will find rest for your souls. Matthew 11:28-29 NIV

Whoever dwells in the shelter of the Most High will rest in the shadow of the Almighty. Psalm 91:1 NIV

DEAR CONFIDENT GIRL,

You CAN have confidence and be confident in Me! I know that very often you have not felt confident. In fact, the very opposite is true. But let's think about why that is true. There have been times when others have "written" things upon your life. And sometimes those things have been terrible and so very wrong. Also, you compare yourself to the world's standards of beauty and worth. Those images you see are not even real! All this has stolen your confidence. Oh how the evil one revels in this. How he uses it to taunt you and tell you that you could never accomplish anything and that you have no reason to be confident. That evil liar! Remember My girl that he comes to kill, steal, and destroy. He wants to steal your confidence. But he has no right! Your confidence is IN Me! I tell you who you are and you are Mine!

- You can be confident in who you are, and Whose you are.
- You can be confident in your salvation if you have believed in and confessed My Son.
- You can be confident in your future.
- You can be confident in My love for you.
- You can be confident in My plans for you.
- You can be confident in all the promises that you see in My word.
- You can be confident that you can do all things through Christ who strengthens you.

Put your confidence where it belongs My girl, in Me! Then believe everything I say about My love for you, your value, and worth in My word. Your confidence should soar like never before My princess; precious daughter of the King!

So much love from,

Your Mighty King and your Father

I can do all things through Christ who strengthens me. Philippians 4:13 NKJV

But blessed is the one who trusts in the LORD, whose confidence is in him. Jeremiah 17:7 NIV

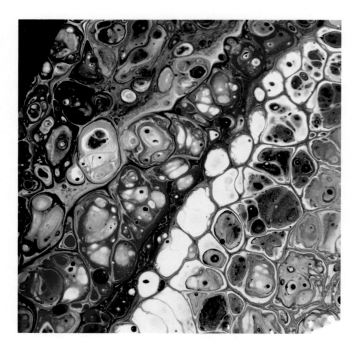

DEAR CALM GIRL,

A simple definition of the word calm is: stillness, tranquility, peaceful, quiet, freedom from motion, unagitated, undisturbed... My girl, can you claim any of the actions or definitions above as your own? Are you calm? Still? Tranquil, quiet, free from motion, agitation or disturbance? Or are you a whirling dervish: wild, irritable, loud, agitated and rushed? Are you always going somewhere and doing something, never quiet, still, tranquil or calm? Do you enjoy living like that? Do you know that you don't have to live this way and it is possible to change? I have something better for you My girl, I always have something better for you, a better way: a quiet heart and mind. A rested body and spirit. Peace and calmness for your soul. Do you believe that I AM who I say I AM? Do you believe in My word? Do you believe that the whole natural world is under My control? Have you not read how I calmed the storms or how the wind and the mighty waves are in My control? My precious child, all these things I can do and so much more! You can trust in My love and protection. That in itself should allow you to be calm. Do not let the world and how it behaves with all its rushing and worrying and success driven lifestyle dictate how you feel and behave. Come to My word early and often. Sit at My feet and learn and trust and enjoy My presence. Let My calmness rule over your heart and soul My child.

So much love from,

The Maker of the wind and waves

47

And he awoke and rebuked the wind and said to the sea, "Peace! Be still!" And the wind ceased, and there was a great calm. Mark 4:39 NKJV

For the LORD your God is living among you. He is a mighty Savior. He will take delight in you with gladness. With his love, he will calm all your fears. He will rejoice over you with joyful songs. Zephaniah 3:17 NLT

Be careful, keep calm and don't be afraid. Do not lose heart... Isaiah 7: 4a NIV

The LORD himself will fight for you. Just stay calm. Exodus 14:14 NLT

"LORD, help!" they cried in their trouble, and he saved them from their distress. He calmed the storm to a whisper and stilled the waves. What a blessing was that stillness as he brought them safely into harbor! Psalm 107:28-30 NLT

"Calm your anger and abandon wrath. Don't be angry— it only leads to evil." Psalm 37:8 ISV

DEAR WORRIED AND ANXIOUS GIRL,

My daughter, I AM in control. Stop and ponder that right now... Insert your biggest worries right here _____ and then say: "My God is in control of _____". "It's your job to pray and Mine to handle the situation. I made the heavens and earth and everything in them, on them and surrounding them. I am in control of the wind and the waves. Do you honestly think that I don't know what's going on with you and surrounding you right now? I know your past, your future and your life right this minute. I know every second, down to the minutest detail. I know. I care. And I am in control. Did you forget that I know the plans I have for you, plans to prosper you and not to harm you, plans to give you a hope and a future? Nothing is a surprise to Me, My child. And I can handle this problem in your life and in the world. Your part, your job is to come to me. Come to me all of you that are weary and carry heavy burdens and I will give you rest. This does not say 'might' give you rest. Your part is to come to Me. My part is to give you the rest you need. This does not mean that I will pluck you out of your trials, burdens, hardships or this partic-ular storm in your life. It does not mean that you will never grieve and your life will be easy and without trouble. You live in a fallen and broken world. The evil one is hard at work here. BUT, The victory has already been won! Jesus is your salvation! Never forget that "greater is he that is in you, then he that is in the world." And "in this world you WILL have trouble, but take heart, I have overcome the world." The antidote for worry is trust. The answer to being weary and anxious is to come to Me, and rest in Me. Come to Me in prayer. Come to My word. Sing My Praise songs! Do these things multiple times a day. I have an endless supply of peace and rest for you My faith-filled girl.

Love from,

The Prince of Peace

> "For I know the plans I have for you ", declares the LORD, " plans to prosper you and not to harm you, plans to give you hope and a future." Jeremiah 29:11 NIV

> Come to Me, all you who labor and are heavy–laden and overburdened, and I will cause you to rest. [I will ease and relieve and refresh your souls.] Matthew 11:28 AMPC

DEAR ROOTED GIRL,

Are you planted firmly in My Truth, Word and Way? Are your toes digging down into the principles of My word? Let your roots grow down into Me. Let your life be built on Me. "Then your faith will grow strong in the truth you were taught, and you will overflow with thankfulness." Don't sit or stand on the complacent, shifting sands. You need a Rock foundation and strong roots. I am that foundation and your roots belong in Me. I am your Rock, Root, Strength, and Peace. I am a Strong Foundation and The Truth. I am Love and Justice. I am The Vine and you are the branches. If your branches stay attached to Me– to live, dwell and abide in Me, then you are connected to My root system and you will live, grow, produce and thrive. Apart from Me you can do nothing. A branch without roots will very quickly die. But a branch attached to the strongest, healthiest, most vibrant Vine, will thrive! You need Me for life. It's an easy formula; No roots= death. Deep roots= life and health and growth and fruit.

You grow girl!

Abba, The Vine

> Let your roots grow down into him, and let your lives be built on him. Then your faith will grow strong in the truth you were taught, and you will overflow with thankfulness.
> Colossians 2:7 NLT

Yes, I am the vine; you are the branches. Those who remain in me, and I in them, will produce much fruit. For apart from me you can do nothing. John 15:5 NLT

Anyone who listens to my teaching and follows it is wise, like a person who builds a house on solid rock. Matthew 7:24 NLT

DEAR GROWING GIRL,

My dear girl, are you growing? Are you rooted in my word? If you are mine, you should always be growing. Your roots should be planted deep within My word and My Son. I am The Vine and you are the branches, remain in Me and I will remain in you. It is my desire that you produce much fruit. To remain means to: live, dwell, abide. If you live in Me and I live in you, you will be growing, you will be thriving and then yes you will be producing fruit. Don't just survive: thrive! Don't have rotten roots, leaves falling off or be a stunted plant! A living, thriving plant does not have these problems. Be as a palm tree or cedar taking in the nourishment of food (My Word) and (living) water. Then, and only then can you be thriving, flourishing, growing, blooming, and producing... A living plant, like a living life needs sunlight, clean air, water, and nourishing soil. A tree needs all these factors. If one or all of them are missing, first the tree will become sick and then eventually will die. A Christian needs; Son-light. Jesus is the light of the world. His word is a lamp to our feet and a light to our path. He can give us living water and his word is our bread of life and sustenance. Are you growing my girl? Life – means: growth. Never stop growing! I love you precious, thriving, growing daughter.

From The Giver of Life,

God

But the godly will flourish like palm trees and grow strong like the cedars of Lebanon. For they are transplanted to the LORD's own house. They flourish in the courts of our God. Even in old age they will still produce fruit; they will remain vital and green. They will declare, "The LORD is just! He is my rock! There is no evil in him!" Psalm 92:12- 15 NLT

DEAR BLOOMING GIRL,

Bloom wherever you are planted My daughter! It is indeed possible to bloom in harsh circumstances and lands. Flowers can and do bloom in freezing temperatures and in some of the hottest places on earth. There are flowers that bloom in forests, with low light and flowers that thrive and bloom in full and constant sun. There are also flowers that bloom at very high and cold altitudes and those that bloom in very low and hot deserts… Also I made hundreds of thousands of species of flowers! Why am I telling you all of this? I love beauty and flowers and I have given both of these to you as gifts. But the reason I specifically told you this is about the comparison: flowers bloom in difficult circumstances and places and you can too! To bloom is to thrive. A plant that is not thriving will usually not bloom. If you are following My word and living each day in My peace and purpose, your life should be blooming and flowering. Will others look at you and see a reflection of Me? Do they see beauty in your life and contentment because you're living for Me, in My will and way? Be a reflection of Me, My beautiful blooming girl. In order for there to be fruit, there must first be blossoms. In order for flowers, the plant must be healthy and nourished. Bloom wherever I have planted you my most beautiful flower. Spread my love with your beautiful spirit and fragrance…

So much love from your,

Master Gardener

So all of us who have had that veil removed can see and reflect the glory of the Lord. And the Lord—who is the Spirit—makes us more and more like him as we are changed into his glorious image. 2 Corinthians 3:18 NLT

Look at the lilies and how they grow. They don't work or make their clothing, yet Solomon in all his glory was not dressed as beautifully as they are. Luke 12:27 NLT

When he went into the Tabernacle of the Covenant the next day, he found that Aaron's staff, representing the tribe of Levi, had sprouted, budded, blossomed, and produced ripe almonds! Numbers 17:8 NLT

DEAR SPENT GIRL,

Do you feel 'spent'? Used up? Maybe even that all the best years of your life are past? Nothing to look forward to? I have come that you might have life! Not a dreaded life, not a meager life, and not a used up and 'over' life. But life to the full! Blooming, brimming over, beautiful, thriving, joyful and useful! There is no one on earth that is exactly like you. I made you with talents, personality and a life's purpose. When you are wounded, sick, struggling, in pain physically or emotionally, it is easy to lose sight of that purpose. I will remind you. I will always be there to remind you. Do not give into the evil one who comes to kill, steal and destroy. Turn to Me. Pray to Me. Glorify Me with your life. I can and will give you the tools you need to accomplish that. You are fully equipped spiritually in Christ Jesus. Look to Me for your purpose and your strength. Remember that I have living water and daily bread! Instead of having a 'spent' or used up life, you will be useful, fresh and renewed! I love you, My useful, fresh and renewed girl!

From,

The Fountain of Life, Your God

> Even youths grow tired and weary, and young men stumble and fall; but those who hope in the Lord will renew their strength. They will soar on wings as eagles; they will run and not grow weary, they will walk and not faint.
> Isaiah 40:30-31 NIV

I will most gladly spend and be spent for your souls. If I love you more, am I to be loved less? 2 Corinthians 12:15 ESV

I replied, "Buy my work seems so useless! I have spent my strength for nothing and to no purpose. Yet I leave it all in the LORD's hand; I will trust God for my reward. Isaiah 49:4 NLT

DEAR BUSY GIRL,

Busy, busy, busy, doing, doing, rushing, proving, busy, comparing, striving, wanting, spinning on a hamster wheel of never ending "to do" lists, wants and obligations. What are you trying to prove? Who are you trying to impress? It would be easier, and a shorter list if I asked who you were not trying to impress. Maybe it's yourself, coworkers, your spouse or family. I know something though; it's not Me. You are not trying to impress or please Me. My girl, you live in a world where you are constantly told you must do this or accomplish that or your kids must play all the different sports, music lessons etc. and that you can handle everything and it's not a problem. There is a problem. A huge problem. There is something missing and you cannot handle it all. You were not designed to do so. Aren't you tired My girl? Tired of the day in, day out striving for what does not matter, does not last and cannot satisfy? I have not asked for this busy life for you. I have asked you to come away with Me, to rest, to pray and live My way, to learn from My word and have a bountiful life. I'm asking you to quit striving for the approval of man. I'm asking you to quit working to appear perfect and like you have it all together. We both know the truth about that! Why do the standards of this world and how others think of you mean so much? If you could only fathom that in the scope of eternity, this earthly life would not even register as a dot. Not a single dot! Does it not make sense then to work for what will last? The opposite of busy is still, quiet. Be still and know that I am God! 'Be still' here can be translated as "cease striving" or "let go, relax".

When you read those words doesn't it make you want to take a deep breath, fall into My arms and rest? I am here for you My girl. Cease striving and store up for yourself treasures in heaven!

Everlasting love from,

The God of eternity.

> Be still and know that I am God; I will be exalted among the nations, I will be exalted in the earth!" Psalm 46:10 ESV

> "Do not lay up for yourselves treasures on earth, where moth and rust destroy and where thieves break in and steal, But store up for yourselves treasures in heaven, where moth and rust do not destroy, and where thieves do not break in and steal. For where your treasure is, there your heart will be also. Matthew 6:19-21 BSB

> But I have calmed and quieted my soul, like a weaned child with its mother; like a weaned child is my soul within me. Psalm 131:2 ESV

DEAR CREATING GIRL,

When you create, you are a reflection of Me. I made everything on this earth and in the heavens above. Things you cannot see, even fathom, or cannot comprehend. I made them all. So when you make something, a drawing, painting, plant a garden, cook a wonderful meal, take a beautiful photograph, or make something beautiful, you are reflecting Me. I know you've been told different things in the past but I want you to believe Me. You creating = reflecting your Creator. People think art and doing something creative is "an extra". Meaning you may do that when all of your "regular" work is done. It's not an aside, but a need I've created in you. Why do you think it fulfills you and gives you such pleasure and joy to make something? It's because I put that in need into you. When you create, you are using one of my characteristics! It gives you joy because I put that need into you. Create My girl, and feel no shame or guilt for taking the time and energy to do so! It is one of My beautiful gifts to you!

Love, from your,

Creator

> So whether you eat or drink, or whatever you do, do it all for the glory of God. 1 Corinthians 10:31 NLT

> Then the Lord said to Moses, "Look, I have specifically chosen Bezalel son of Uri, grandson of Hur, of the tribe of Judah. I have filled him with the spirit of God, giving him

great wisdom, ability, and expertise in all kinds of crafts. He is a master craftsman (artisan) expert in working with gold, silver, and bronze. He is skilled in engraving and mounting gemstones and in engraving wood. He is master at every craft! Exodus 31:1-5 NIV

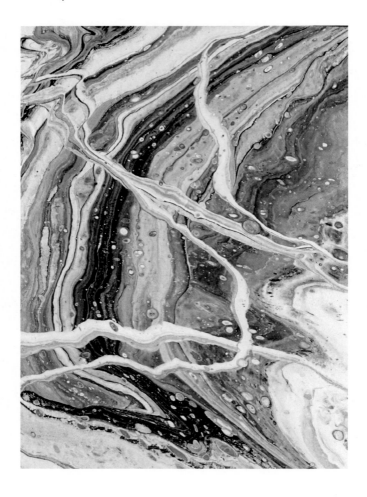

DEAR POSSIBLE GIRL,

Do you know that anything is possible if a person believes? Anything. Believes. These words are very important but what is even more important is that you know The Who and where this comes from. On your own it is impossible, but with Me, all things are possible. Do you believe that? Do you remember that without faith it is impossible to please Me? Now it may seem as a play on words, but it is not and it is really quite simple:

- On your own, things are not possible.
- With Me anything is possible.
- You must believe &
- You must have faith

So go forward My possible daughter, believing with great faith. Remember that with Me nothing is impossible! Live in My will and your possibilities then are endless!

So much love from your,

Almighty God Who makes all things possible!

> Jesus said to him, "As far as possibilities go, everything is possible for the person who believes." Mark 9:23 GWT

> Looking at them Jesus said, "With people [as far as it depends on them] it is impossible, but not with God; for all things are possible with God." Mark 10:27 AMP

"For nothing will be impossible with God." Like 1:37 ESV

I can do all things through Christ who strengthens me.
Philippians 4:13 NKJV

MY DEAR TRUTHFUL DAUGHTER,

It is imperative that you tell the truth. That is a strong word, but I can't emphasize enough how important this is for your life. For every day. Every moment. Satan is a liar and the father of all lies. I am Truth. You have no business speaking or believing what the liar tells you! You know that the evil one wants to kill, steal and destroy. He wants to ruin relationships, families, marriages, and beliefs about who you are. But you are a daughter of The King! You are a daughter of hope and truth and love. Believe what I say and what I think of you! Use your armor! Is your belt of truth buckled? Are you even wearing it? The truth is what heals you. My truth. The truth of My Word. My word shows you how to live. And teaches you what to do, what to say, and not say and how much I love you! In My truth there is freedom and healing! Believe what I say and what I think of you. Use your armor. You cannot fight without protection. Go forward living in truth, speaking the truth, being honest in all things and sharing that with others. Do not forget that the evil one will try to convince you of the opposite of how I say to live and how much I love you. Do not believe him!

Stay alert.

Stay guarded.

Stay armed.

Stay conscious.

Stay calm.

Stay hopeful.

Stay in my love.

Be honest.

Live in my truth!

I love you so much my truthful daughter…

From, The Truth

The LORD detests lying lips, but he delights in those who tell the truth. Proverbs 12:22 NLT

The entirety of Your word is truth, and all Your righteous judgments endure forever. Proverbs 119:160 BSB

Jesus said to him, "I am the way, and the truth, and the life. No one comes to the Father except through me. Proverbs 14:6 ESV

Paul, a servant of God and an apostle of Jesus Christ to further the faith of God's elect and their knowledge of the truth that leads to godliness— in the hope of eternal life, which God, who does not lie, promised before the beginning of time, Titus 1:1-2 NIV

DEAR ENSLAVED GIRL,

And now I am getting 'controversial', in man's eyes anyway. I must speak the truth; there are things, habits and relationships that are 'holding you captive'. You may very well live in a free world and the word 'enslaved' actually offends you. But again I speak the truth to you because I love you and because it is My desire for you to be free! There are false prophets and teachers among you. Think beyond just teachers but also the lies about Me everywhere and the lies that everything in this world is OK to do. Lies can be so subtle, so appealing – they are broadcast right in front of you in so many forms. But they are false! My word is the truth! My Son is The Truth, the way and the Life! That is why I want your freedom My girl! These wrong things may appeal and distract and give pleasure for a moment, but with what are you left? Emptiness and shame. A continual need for more. What I offer is beautiful and fresh. It leaves you wanting to praise Me and with a true feeling of joy unspeakable and full of glory. It is a choice to be enslaved to this world and the things of this world, to live in shame or with shame and agony and frustration. Or you can do what I tell you to do or not do in My word. With another word; it's called obedience! So live in peace and freedom! It's possible my girl. With true and genuine love.

From,

Your God of freedom

But there were also false prophets among the people, just as there will be false teachers among you. They will secretly introduce destructive heresies, even denying the sovereign Lord who bought them—bringing swift destruction on themselves. 2 Peter 2:1 NIV

Because of the weakness of your human nature, I am using the illustration of slavery to help you understand all this. Previously, you let yourselves be slaves to impurity and lawlessness, which led ever deeper into sin. Now you must give yourselves to be slaves to righteous living so that you will become holy. Romans 6:19 NLT

They promise freedom, but they themselves are slaves of sin and corruption. For you are a slave to whatever controls you. 2 Peter 2:19 NLT

DEAR HIDING GIRL,

My Dear Girl, there is no need to hide anymore. I know you. I know your past. You have asked for forgiveness for wrong choices, paths, decisions, and actions. And I have forgiven you. That is how My love and grace works. I forgive you because of My Son's sacrifice and your request for forgiveness, my mercy, grace and who I Am. But My girl, when I forgive, it is forever! I never look at your sin again, can't see your sin and know that they are thrown away as far as the east is from the west. They are covered with My Son's blood. Washed white as snow. Done. Finished. Complete. Why are you walking around with these heavy burdens on your shoulders? Don't you know that you don't need to carry them at all? If you have asked for My forgiveness, you are free! Walk free. There's no need to hang your head in shame. No need to hide from Me or others. I have turned your "hiding" into "hidden". You are protected and hidden in Me. The one word, hiding; brings up shame and the other word, hidden; protection. You were hidden in and by the Rock of your salvation. I cover you with My feathers and you are hidden under the shadow of My wings. Your salvation is sure. Your forgiveness is complete. Your name is in My book and your forever residence is in heaven- reserved, deposit paid, and secure. Walk with your head held high, daughter of the most high King!

I love you,

The Rock of your salvation

He will call out to me; you are my father, my God, the rock of my salvation. Psalm 89:26 NIV

He will cover you with his feathers. He will shelter you with his wings. His faithful promises are your armor and protection. Psalm 91:4 NLT

For you died and your life is now hidden with Christ in God. Colossians 3:3 NIV

You are my hiding place; you will protect me from trouble and surround me with songs of deliverance. Psalm 32:7 NIV

How abundant are the good things that you have stored up for those who fear you, that you bestow in the sight of all, on those who take refuge in you. In the shelter of your presence you hide them from all human intrigues; you keep them safe in your dwelling from accusing tongues. Psalm 31:19-20 NIV

You are my hiding place and my shield; I put my hope in Your word. Psalm 119:114 BSB

DEAR TRUSTING GIRL,

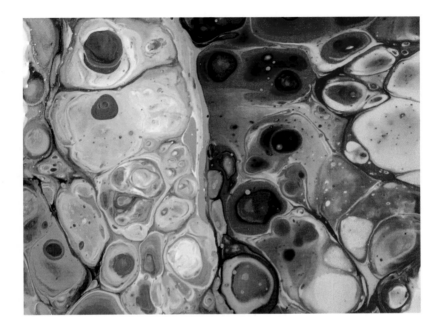

Do you trust Me My girl? Do you truly trust Me? If you believe in Me, believe in My Son's Life, death, burial and resurrection, you are a person of faith. Faith takes trust. You need to have trust to believe. So if you believe that I AM Who I say I AM and that I AM The Creator of all things... And you Believe that the Bible is My Word and believe what it says about Me... and believes what it tells you that I think and say about you... If all that is the case and you believe all of that, you are a trusting girl. You are a girl of faith. So, when hard times come (and they will), When you have questions or question Me (and you will)... this is the exact time to exercise that trust. If I want what's best for you and I absolutely do, then you have to trust, believe and have faith that I will work things out for you and for your very best. It doesn't mean that you'll be able to see what I'm doing or the way I do it or the timing of it, but you can trust in My plan for you. Trusting is an exercise, And the more you exercise your trust, the stronger your trust becomes. It's like a limb or muscle you want to strengthen, you must exercise it, do the work, increase the weight and repetitions. It will become stronger and increase in size the more it is used! You know Me. You believe Me. You believe in and read My Word. Exercise your trust muscles My girl and increase in your faith!

So much love from,

You're trustworthy God and Father

> Trust in the Lord with all your heart. Do not depend on your own understanding. Seek his will in all you do and he will show you which path to take. Proverbs 3:5-6 (NLT)

> For I know the plans I have for you declares the Lord. Plans to prosper you and not to harm you. Plans to give you hope and a future. Jeremiah 29:11

DEAR FORGIVEN GIRL,

My dear forgiven daughter. I have forgiven you. When will you accept that? I know that you have made wrong choices at times. I know that you have done things you knew were wrong. I know that you have hurt others, slandered others and at times even hated them. But I also know that all of these things and more have been done to you. Do you really think I'm in heaven looking down on you because you are so imperfect? Do you really believe I don't know that you have a fallible human body and mind? I know that you live in a broken world, many times with a broken body and spirit. Do you have any idea of the extent of my love and mercy for you my daughter? If you did, you would know that I have forgiven you! Why do you think that I sent my only beloved Son to wash away your sins? When you come to me and ask forgiveness my child, you are forgiven you are washed white as snow and your sins are cast as far as the east is from the west. I don't even remember them anymore. Why are you letting memories of them torture you? You agonize and regret and ask forgiveness over and over again. Do you think this comes from me? It does not. It is a tool of Satan. He comes to kill, steal and destroy. When he does this with sin memories, he is trying to steal your peace of mind and joy. He's trying to destroy your trust in me and my word. Rebuke him in Jesus name! Name! I have forgiven and it is in the past. My spirit gently nudges you when I want to warn you or teach you. The evil one causes you to agonize and shames you. Believe me. Believe my word. Believe in my son. Believe in the cross and resurrection. Believe in my mercy and forgiveness! It's once and for always! I love you my forgiven daughter.

Your,

Ever merciful God.

> Blesses in the one whose transgressions are forgiven, whose sins are covered. Psalm 32:1 NIV

> Oh, what joy for those whose disobedience is forgiven, whose sins are put out of sight. Romans 4:7 NLT

> He has removed our sins as far from us as the east is from the west. Psalm 103:12 NLT

DEAR WARRIOR GIRL,

My dear girl, My word tells you that you are strong in the Lord and in the power of his might! That's My might! That makes you mighty strong and powerful indeed! But did you notice that this verse says, Be strong IN THE LORD and IN the Power of HIS MIGHT? Your strength and power come from Me. Be wise and always remember this. Now, are you wearing your armor? You are going to battle every single day so you definitely need to be wearing your armor, your protection! A warrior needs her armor! Do you have that belt of truth wrapped around you? Truth is your foundation. All My words are true. My Son is the way, the truth and the life. If truth is My character and My Son is the Truth, which it is and He is, do you think it matters to Me if you are truthful? Of course it does! Let truth be at your center as the belt of truth encircles you. Now, the breastplate of righteousness. You have the righteousness of Christ. The breastplate protects your heart and other vital organs. Physically speaking without your heart, pumping blood, oxygen and blood cells to every other organ, system and cell in your body, you would be gone within a matter of minutes. If you are going to battle, you must have your special battle shoes on. They have spikes and will help you stand firm. You must stand your ground and not fall. But are you wondering why we are talking about armor and battles and then say that you are supposed to wear shoes that signify the 'Gospel of Peace'? Remember that you are to bring the message of My Son Jesus to the world. He is the Prince of peace. His message is peace. The evil one does not want peace for you, or anyone else in this world. That's why you must stand. That's why you must be prepared and ready. Now I want you to picture that shield in front of you, protecting you from incoming arrows. That shield is faith; what you believe. And if you believe that I am God Almighty, Maker and sustainer of the universe, and that I sent My Son, My only Son Jesus to come to earth to live as your example, to die for your sins, and that he rose again on the third day… If you know/believe/trust this; what a mighty, amazing and protecting shield you have! The devil will constantly try to fool you with lies! That shield will protect you. Next we have the helmet of salvation. Salvation is integral, the basis of you being My child. When you believe in Me and My Son, that helmet of salvation is the protection of the center of your intellect: your head, your mind, your brain, your emotions, thought processes and decision making. It is imperative that it is covered and protected. This is where the evil one will try and attack you the most! Your physical brain also controls movement, breathing, heart regulation, and every other autonomic function. One swift blow, jab, thrust or explosion can take you out, wound you greatly and cause great harm. What can you do without your ability to think and feel? What would happen if a dangerous enemy was in charge of both your heart and mind? It would be extremely dangerous of course because that enemy could completely control you! And make no mistake my girl, do not be fooled; that is exactly what the evil one is striving to do to you: Every•Single•Day. Now for your sword! It is your only offensive weapon and what an incredible weapon it is! The sword of the Spirit, My Spirit, is Me with you at all times! You can do what you need to do in My strength. Do not try to fight on your own or give up because the battle is fierce or long. You are My soldier, My warrior daughter, and I am with you at all times and will strengthen, help and protect you. And then what do you do with all of these weapons of war? Because make no mistake, this life is a war, and the battle with the evil rulers of the power of the air, is very real. To pretend it is not is to leave yourself completely unprepared and unprotected. After you are covered with all of this protection and you have your sword ready, what else do you do? You walk forward, ready and prepared. You fight evil and be an example of peace! You put one foot in front of the other, day in, day out. Live in My peace. Be an example of My peace. Bring My peace to this very troubled world and needy population. And never, ever forget to pray, pray, pray!

Be prepared.

Be vigilant.

Stay protected My Girl.

Stand your ground!

So much love,

From your Commander and Protector

All your words are true; all your righteous laws are eternal. Psalm 119:160 NIV

Finally, be strong in the Lord and in his mighty power. Put on the full armor of God, so that you can take your stand against the devil's schemes. For our struggle is not against flesh and blood, but against the rulers, against the authorities, against the powers of this dark world and against the spiritual forces of evil in the heavenly realms. Therefore put on the full armor of God, so that when the day of evil comes, you may be able to stand your ground, and after you have done everything, to stand. Stand firm then, with the belt of truth buckled around your waist, with the breastplate of righteousness in place, and with your feet fitted with the readiness that comes from the gospel of peace. In addition to all this, take up the shield of faith, with which you can extinguish all the flaming arrows of the evil one. Take the helmet of salvation and the sword of the Spirit, which is the word of God. And pray in the Spirit on all occasions with all kinds of prayers and requests. With this in mind, be alert and always keep on praying for all the Lord's people. Ephesians 6:10-18 NIV

For the word of God is living and active, sharper than any two-edged sword, piercing to the division of soul and of spirit, of joints and of marrow, and discerning the thoughts and intentions of the heart. Hebrews 4:12 ESV

Peace I leave with you; my peace I give you. I do not give to you as the world gives. Do not let your hearts be troubled and do not be afraid. John 14:27 NIV

DEAR JUDGED GIRL,

They think they know you. They think they have you all figured out. They think they have a right. But they don't. You are My child. And I know you. I know your heart. I also know your story, your past, your wounds, your worries, your motives, your pain, and absolutely everything about you. I know how others have hurt you and judged you. But who are they to judge? How can they see past the log in their own eye to point out the splinter in yours? There is only One Judge and that is Me. But I am not as the world sees Me. I am just. I am loving. I am kind. I am merciful. I am love. I have you engraved on the palms of My hands. I chose you, yes you before I made the world to be in My family! And do you know that it delighted me, gave me great pleasure to do so? My child, does that sound like a God, a Judge, a heavenly father that is out to 'get' you? Is that a God, your God, that is just looking for your faults, failings and how to strike you down? Not so My child! Search Me out in My word, My natural world, and in prayer. If you search for Me with all your heart I will be found by you! Now, about those other "judges"… Why do they do it? They want to feel better about themselves, point out someone else's faults and flaws, or even perceived faults, so they can feel proud of their own righteousness. Sometimes, it's because they are jealous. But righteousness comes from My Son, not from what they can do or accomplish. Another thing My girl, it's not even up to you to judge yourself. If you have done something wrong, said something wrong, bring it to Me. I will forgive you My girl and never look on it nor remember it again.

Forgive those who persecute you, be merciful and love them. I am not saying they deserve this. But just telling you the best, healthiest and righteous way to live. Because I love you, yes you, so much!

Your Righteous, Merciful, and loving Judge

You hypocrite, first take the log out of your own eye, and then you will see clearly to take the speck out of your brother's eye. Matthew 7:5 ESV

See, I have engraved you on the palms of my hands; your walls are ever before me. Isaiah 49:16 NIV

Even before he made the world, God loved us and chose us in Christ to be holy and without fault in his eyes. God decided in advance to adopt us into his own family by bringing us to himself through Jesus Christ. This is what he wanted to do, and it gave him great pleasure. Ephesians 1:4-5 NLT

You will seek me and find me when you seek me with all your heart. Jeremiah 29:13 NIV

And because of him you are in Christ Jesus, who became to us wisdom from God, righteousness and sanctification and redemption, so that, as it is written, "Let the one who boasts, boast in the Lord." 1 Corinthians 1:30-31 ESV

I care very little if I am judged by you or by any human court; indeed, I do not even judge myself. My conscience is clear, but that does not make me innocent. It is the Lord who judges me. 1 Corinthians 4:3-4 NIV

DEAR BROKEN-HEARTED GIRL,

Oh My girl! Your heart is broken. So very broken and crushed. It feels like it has been ripped open by a sword and you don't know how it could possibly ever be fixed or healed again. You question if life will ever be "normal" for you again… And if you will ever be able to smile or laugh… Or will these tears ever stop? You question if I love you, if I see your pain and even how I could allow such grief in your life… And you don't see how you can go on, in fact you don't want to.… But I am here My child. I do see. I do care. So much more than you will ever know. My heart is touched by your grief! How can a loving God, you ask, allow such things to happen to his own child? Why is there such pain and unspeakable evil on this earth? My precious little child, There is so much you will never know while you dwell on this earth. My ways are not your ways, and my thoughts are not your thoughts. You cannot understand and I ask that you just trust me and have faith. The evil one will receive his payment for all the evil he has done. There will be justice for you my girl and your reward will be to be with Me for all eternity. Can you think of that? Joy unspeakable and full of glory! You cannot even imagine all that I have stored up for you! In the meantime, come to me constantly, cry out to me, stay in my word and pray pray pray! Take a step each day. It doesn't matter how small. Allow others that love you and have walked a road similar to yours help you. Ask for help. I will hear you! I am holding you in my arms... I will bind up those wounds, wipe your tears away. Heal you and comfort you. I have not forsaken you. I•adore•you!

From,

Your Healer

> The LORD is close to the brokenhearted and saves those who are crushed in spirit. Psalm 34:18 NIV

> A cheerful heart is good medicine, but a broken spirit saps a person's strength. Proverbs 7:22 NLT

> He heals the brokenhearted and binds up their wounds. Psalms 147:3 NLT

DEAR TRUSTING GIRL 2,

I could address this as: Dear Fretting Girl, But I prefer in this letter to focus again on trusting. In Psalm 37 verses one through five, I begin with what you should not do; Fret or be envious. Fret is an 'old fashioned' word in this year 2021 and not one you use or think of unless you see it in Scripture. But its meaning is very important! Some Bible versions translate this word as "worry" or "become angry", but let's go back to "fret". This tiny word has a large and eye-opening definition. To fret is to feel or express worry, annoyance or discontent. It also means to cause erosion, gnaw into something, corrosion and wearing away. Now think in terms of that word and your body, mind, heart, spirit and emotions. This worry, annoyance and discontent leads to all of the above, (body, mind, heart, spirit and emotions): to erode, wear away and corrode. Let me ask you this: does any worry, envy or frustration about others cause them to stop what they are doing or how they are behaving? No. A resounding, capital -NO! So why do it? Instead, I ask that you do what My following versus tell you to do: Verses 3 through 6 say-Trust in the Lord, and do good; dwell in the land and cultivate faithfulness. Delight yourself in the Lord; and he will give you the desires of your heart. Commit your way to the LORD, trust also in him and He will do it. Two-'do nots', Seven-'dos' and 2- 'He wills') I tell you what not to do: fret and be envious – for your own health; those things cause you to corrode and wear way. I tell you seven things to do: trust, do good, dwell, cultivate, delight, commit and trust. Anchored and completed with trust on both sides.

And then what My girl? I WILL DO IT. Trust in My Word, My way and that I will do it, I will complete it! I cannot and will not go back on My word. If I have said it, you can totally trust that I will do it!

So much love from,

Your Trustworthy and Completing Father

> Who of you by worrying can add a single hour to your life? Since you cannot do this very little thing, why do you worry about the rest? Like 12:25-26 NIV

> Trust in the LORD with all your heart; do not depend on your own understanding. Seek his will in all you do, and he will show you which path to take. Don't be impressed with your own wisdom. Instead, fear the LORD and turn away from evil. Proverbs 3:5-7 NLT

DEAR HONORING GIRL,

I want you to know that it is right for you to honor Me. I AM The LORD Almighty, The One and Only God. I want you to learn early on to have reverence for Me. Put Me and My will first in all you do. Honor My Son and My Word and do not grieve the Holy Spirit. The first way you should learn to know Me is through My word. You have the very words of your Father God in a book. Wouldn't it make sense for you to read this book, study it and learn from it? In fact, you should treasure it! Another way you can know Me more and learn more about Me is by learning My names and what they mean. I have many special names and I want you to know them so they will comfort you throughout your life. Search them out in My word and study them. Here are just a few...I Am your Creator, your LORD God, your Supplier, your Master, your Provider, your Healer, your great Physician , your Banner, your Sanctifier, and your Savior! Learn these names my child and it will bless you to be able to call Me; my Creator, my LORD God, my Supplier, my Master, my Provider, my Healer, my Banner, my Sanctifier, and my Great Physician. So have a deep respect for Me, The Most High and Holy God. There are many ways that you can honor Me, My child; with your words, your actions, your thoughts, your heart, your attitude and your gratitude. My word tells you to love Me with all your heart, mind, soul and strength. When you love Me like that and I have the first place in your life and when you know, truly know that I Am The Holy God, then honoring Me is not a difficult task, but a beautiful, right, peaceful and honoring way to live. I love you, My honoring girl.

Your,

Loving Father and your Most Holy God.

> Lord, how wonderful you are! You have stored up so many good things for us, like a treasure chest heaped up and spilling over with blessings—all for those who honor and worship you!Everybody knows what you can do for those who turn and hide themselves in you. Psalm 31:19 TPT

> He answered, "Love the Lord your God with all your heart and with all your soul and with all your strength and with all your mind'; and, 'Love your neighbor as yourself.' Luke 10:27 NIV

> Your word I have treasured in my heart, That I may not sin against You. Psalm 119:11 NAS

DEAR RADIANT GIRL,

My dear bright, light-filled, beaming, vivid, luminous, glowing, sparkly, and radiant daughter! Those who look to Me are radiant; their faces are never covered with shame. Do you know what this word radiant means? The definitions in Hebrew, Greek and English are so stunning that they will surprise and delight you. In Hebrew radiant means: emitting or darting rays of light, proceeding as from a Center; light; shining; bright with joy, hope, to shine, be radiant, to burn or sparkle. It is a literal light not a metaphor. In Greek it means to flash forth like lightning! And in English it is emitting rays of light, shining; bright. Bright with joy, hope, etc. Also, from the Webster's 1828 dictionary, Shooting or darting rays of light; beaming with brightness; emitting a vivid light or splendor, as the radiant sun. Isn't that absolutely beautiful? This is how I see you and how I want you to see yourself. Isn't that how you want to live My girl? The looking to Me is the key to living this way and being radiant My daughter. You can only reflect the light you look upon. If you are looking down, your eyes are downcast, as in shame, you can't see the light and you can't reflect the light. Think of a mirror with the sun. Without a source of light, a mirror is dull and lifeless. But when it reflects the sun (The Son), it is blinding! If you would reflect my radiance, you would be able to share that with others. You were made in My image child. Are you remembering that each and every day? You were made to shine! You must first look to The Source of Light in order to be radiant and then be able to reflect that light, and let others see it. Look to Me, My girl! Let go of your shame and be a beaming light for others. You•Glow•Girl! So much love and light

From your,

Resplendent and Blindingly Radiant God.

Those who look to Him for help will be radiant with joy; no shadow of shame will darken their faces. NLT

Those who look to him are radiant; their faces are never covered with shame. Psalm 34:5 NIV

Arise [from spiritual depression to a new life], shine [be radiant with the glory and brilliance of the LORD]; for your light has come, and the glory and brilliance of the LORD has risen upon you. Isiah 60:1 AMP

Therefore be imitators of God, as beloved children; and walk in love, just as Christ also loved you and gave Himself up for us, an offering and a sacrifice to God as a fragrant aroma. Ephesians 5:1-2 NASV

And we, who with unveiled faces all reflect the glory of the Lord, are being transformed into His image with intensifying glory, which comes from the Lord, who is the Spirit. 2 Corinthians 3:18 BSB

The precepts of the Lord are right, making the heart glad; the command of the Lord is radiant, making the eyes light up. Psalm 19:8 HCSB

DEAR DEPRESSED GIRL,

My dear, sad daughter. I am sorry that you are hurting. Do you know that I am close by? I am with you even when you cannot feel Me. I am close to the broken-hearted and save those who are crushed in spirit. Sometimes it helps to remember that there were many people in My word that were downcast, broken-hearted, troubled, miserable, despairing, mourning and hopeless. David, Elijah, Jonah, Job, and Jeremiah all had instances of depression. Even My Son Jesus with his human emotions was called a man of sorrows and acquainted with grief. He was rejected and despised. Before his death, his disciples could not even keep watch with him for one hour and he said, "My soul is deeply grieved to the point of death." Jesus knows how you are feeling! Maybe you have suffered great loss or are grieving a loved one or you are physically ill. Bring your sorrows to Me , My girl. I can carry the load and you also. I can bring help and healing and I am always here with you. My Word is filled with so much hope and comfort. There is a key My girl that might feel impossible when I mention it. But I will anyway. There is power in praise. There is joy in being thankful. And contentment when you put your hope in Me. And very importantly, remember that this life with all its troubles is just a speck on the timeline of eternity. I will wipe every tear from your eyes and there will never be anymore death or sorrow, crying or pain in My heavenly kingdom. Everything will be healed and redeemed and you will have unspeakable joy and be with Me forever. Open your heart to My healing daughter, so you can once again become a joyful girl!

So much love,

from The Great Physician

> He will wipe every tear away from their eyes. There will be no more death or sorrow or crying or pain. All these things are gone forever. Revelation 21:4 NIV

> The LORD is close to the brokenhearted and saves those who are crushed in spirit. Psalm 34:18 NIV

> Why, my soul, are you downcast? Why so disturbed within me? Put your hope in God, for I will yet praise him, my Savior and my God. Psalm 43:5 NIV

DEAR PERSEVERING GIRL,

This means you are: determined, resolute; decided; settled, and resolved. Say it, believe it! Keep at it My girl! Put one foot in front of the other and keep pressing on. Day in, day out. Sometimes it's hourly, or by the minute. But let Me assure you, you can do it, with My help! Be determined to stay strong until the end. This is in your Christian walk and witness. Stick with the how and where and what I am leading you in or to. Be disciplined. If I have put a dream, idea, or plan on your heart and you know it's from me, do it! Do the work! Finish it! Run this race of life with the intention of winning the prize! That will not come instantly or overnight but with much hard work. But the prize is always worth it, isn't it? Just as in doing things My way leaves you with a prize also; peace of mind, companionship with Me, peace and joy in your heart, purpose, and love. Do•not•let•fear•stop•you. Do not let the opinions of others influence you. Do not let the nagging of the evil one deter you. If he is trying to dissuade you from the idea, dream or plan I have put into your heart and mind, you can be sure that he is trying to stop you because he knows the impact this fulfillment will make on your life and on the lives of others. He does not want anything that is good or lovely or healing to transpire. So for that very reason, push through. Go forward. Press on. March with might. And remember that I plan to do good with the outcome. You are strong in the Lord and in the power of his might! You can do it: with Me and through Me. Use your weapons. Do the work. And pray for My help each and every step of the way! You will do it My very determined girl! So much love.

From,

Your resolute Brother Jesus and your very capable Father God.

> I press on toward the goal to win the prize for which God has called me heavenward in Christ Jesus. Philippians 3:14 NIV

> A final word: be strong in the Lord and in his mighty power. Put on all of God's armor so that you will be able to stand firm against all strategies of the devil. Ephesians 6:10-11 NLT

> In addition to all of these, hold up the shield of faith to stop the fiery arrows of the devil. Put on salvation as your helmet, and take the sword of the spirit, which is the word of God. Ephesians 6:16- 17 NLT

> Let perseverance finish its work so that you may be mature and complete, not lacking anything. James 1:4 NIV

DEAR JEALOUS GIRL,

My wonderful, amazing and beautiful daughter. There is no need for you to feel jealousy for anyone else! I have made you one-of-a-kind. You are completely individual and amazing in every right and way. Do you know that it was Me Who knit you together in your mother's womb? I know everything about you, every cell in your body, and every hair on your head. I know your talents, because I gave them to you. I know your struggles, your hopes, your dreams and certainly your disappointments. You are different, special, and unique. Your talents are individual and I made it that way on purpose. I don't make carbon copies. There is a reason for the gifts that you have, that I have given you. Just because someone else, another daughter of mine has accomplishments that you don't necessarily have, that does not make you inferior! Maybe she sings better than you do, has children, has a successful business, a larger house, more money, is a better organizer or is more artistic than you… I could make many comparisons here, but what is the use? She-is-not-you! Period. She does not have the things that you have or the gifts that I have given you! Nothing I do is random or unplanned. I know the plans I have for you, for your life; your talents. It comes down to trust. Do you trust Me? Can you be thankful for what I have given you? Are you willing to cultivate and work hard with the gifts and dreams I have given you? Your life and your talents are indeed gifts from Me. But what are they truly for? To bring you acclaim, money or fame? Or are they to bring honor to My Name? How it would turn your thinking around if you would see it in this manner. If you would remember how incredibly much I love you and that it is Me that you need to look to for your value, purpose and strength, you won't feel inferior or less talented. Use what I have given you! Learn, grow, and expand your talents and use them for My honor and glory. Do not compare My girl! It only steals your joy! Be happy for your sister and her blessings and pray more blessings upon her. When you have those twinges of jealousy, acknowledge them and bring them to Me...

So much love from your,

Maker and gift Giver

> For you created my inmost being; you knit me together in my mother's womb. Psalm 139:13 NIV

> Anger is cruel and fury overwhelming, but who can stand before jealousy? Proverbs 27:4 NIV

> You are still worldly. For since there is jealousy and quarreling among you, are you not worldly? Are you not acting like mere humans? 1 Corinthians 3:3 NIV

DEAR GIFTED GIRL,

My wonderful talented daughter, how I love you! Before you ever came to be I chose the talents that you would have. In other words, I bestowed you with gifts. Many and varied gifts. No one in this world has the exact set of gifts and talents that I chose for you. Maybe you are not pleased with your gifts. Maybe you think you have nothing to offer, or have talents so small that you can't do anything with them. Maybe you wish you had someone else's talents. Now that, you not change and neither will I. I had reasons for what I gave and it is your job to discover what they are, how to grow them and how to use them for My glory. Yes you read that right. You do not have them so others will be impressed with you, or be jealous of you or puff yourself up with pride. All that you are and all that you have is to be used to bring glory to My Name. Any talent you have, no matter how small can be grown. You try, you test, you learn and you grow. You fail at something and you try again. You fall and you get up again. You push forward when you want to give up and eventually you will succeed. Nothing worth having or doing is going to come easily. (Of course, you need My help and direction and strength for all things My girl). In the parable of the talents and the servants, whatever was given, in this instance 'talents', or money, it was expected to be used and grown. One servant hid his talent because he was afraid and actually buried it. Think on those words. He was afraid to use what he was given and was able to add nothing to his talent and therefore had nothing more to give his master. He was called a wicked and lazy servant. Harsh words but they show the gravity of not using what you have been given! You are not starting from scratch. You have been gifted with something, let go of that fear and use it! The world and your Master are looking forward to what you do with your talents My daughter!

From your,

Master God

> To those who use well what they are given, even more will be given, and they will have an abundance. But from those who do nothing, even what little they have will be taken away. Matthew 25:29 NLT

> ...What do you have that God hasn't given you? And if everything you have is from God, why boast as though it were not a gift? 1 Corinthians 4:7 NLT

> As each has received a gift, use it to serve one another, as good stewards of God's varied grace: 1 Peter 4:10 ESV

DEAR ABUNDANT GIRL,

You have because I give. Anything and everything you are or have is a gift from Me. Abundant is: present in high quantity; more than adequate; fully sufficient; plentiful; rich. I have given you life, breath, talent, love, purpose, mercies, grace, My precious only Son Jesus Christ and eternal life. I sent my Son so you would have life and have it abundantly. My child, if that does not sound abundant to you, you need to check your heart. Are you thankful for all these things or is it never enough? It is My desire that you be thankful for all you have been given and that in everything you give thanks; Whether it's something you gladly receive or something that is difficult. Live according to My will, way and Word and you will have abundant joy!

Love from your,

Abundantly Generous God

> The thief comes only to steal and kill and destroy. I came that they may have life and have it abundantly. John 10:10 ESV

> And give thanks for everything to God the Father in the name of our Lord Jesus Christ. Ephesians 5:20 NLT

> You feed them from the abundance of your own house, letting them drink from your river of delights. Psalm 36:8 NLT

DEAR GIVING GIRL,

What a beautiful giving soul you have My precious daughter! How you love to give and serve others. It really is a beautiful thing. And it is a reflection of Me. You are using your gift and that is what I want you to do...But just one little thing I want to mention: every gift is like a double-edged sword. It's a good thing, a very good thing and a gift from Me, but it can also harm you... What does that mean? It means that whatever is your greatest gift, can also become a weakness or thorn in your side. Why is that? Gifts can be misused, overused, obsessed over, or used for pride. Because what I give as a gift, the evil one tries to use against you in harm. There is a saying that every coin has two sides, so it is with your gift. What I give for good, he will try to twist or mess up or use for another outcome or purpose. This is just a warning of precaution for you to be careful. Check with Me on everything. And make sure you really listen when I am giving you the answer. In this instance of your "giving" gift for example, you can burn yourself out by overdoing and not replenishing. Resources need to be replenished. Bodies need to be fed and they need to sleep and they need to be replenished emotionally, physically and especially spiritually. And very importantly, they need to rest! Another thing you need to do is check your motive. Even though you're using your gift in the right way, is there a part of you that is using it to be accepted, loved or thought well of? If you're doing it for Me and in My strength, there's no need to worry about pleasing others. They will be blessed in the process of you using your gift, but it is not about pleasing them. And do not do it because you want to earn My approval. I cannot love you more than I already do because it is not based on your actions. My love is fierce and complete because I am God and you are you. I love you because you are My child, My daughter, and I made you. Do what you do with the strength I give you. You must be filled up with Me and then you will be able to pour out onto others. Ask for My strength and ask who I want you to bless. Do not go above and beyond to be accepted by others or you will only become completely depleted in all areas. I am not asking or suggesting that you stop giving. It is your gift. And it is absolutely beautiful. I'm just reminding you to do it wisely. Give My daughter and do it with and in My strength.

So much love from,

Your Strength and Replenisher, your Holy God and Abba Father!

> Give, and you will receive. Your gift will return to you in full—pressed down, shaken together to make room for more, running over, and poured into your lap. The amount you give will determine the amount you get back. Luke 6:38 NLT

> Each of you should give what you have decided in your heart to give, not reluctantly or under compulsion, for God loves a cheerful giver. And God is able to bless you abundantly, so that in all things at all times, having all that you need, you will abound in every good work. 2 Corinthians 9:6-8 NIV

> As each has received a gift, use it to serve one another, as good stewards of God's varied grace: 1 Peter 4:10 ESV

DEAR HONEY GIRL,

Honey symbolizes richness, prosperity, and abundance. There is a reason that the Promised Land for the Israelites is called, 'The land of milk and honey'. It wasn't just milk and honey, it was flowing. What does the image of something flowing bring to you? It's not dead or stagnant, but has life and moves forward. There is bounty and even excess. Now think of honey flowing, down the side of a jar or from a hive... There is a richness about it, an overabundance, a prosperity. Honey is "an extra". You don't need it to live, like icing on a cake, not necessary but so enjoyable. It is also a delicious, nutritious gift. Extravagant. I didn't just give you bread and water, savory flavors, but I also gave you the extra sweetness of honey! Honey is mentioned in My word in many different ways and many times. In fact, Isaiah even prophesied of My Son eating honey as a child. Honey was also used as a gift, a sign of luxury, delicacy and delight. It was used for health and to give strength, both physically and emotionally. And spiritually honey is used as a comparison to the sweetness of My word. Honey and gold were both used to compare how valuable My word is and how valued it should be. There was both wild honey and farmed honey but let's talk about the wild... With wild honey, a hive must first be located. It needed to be taken from the bees, often high up, sometimes in perilous locations. Then they had to remove it without very many stings. Honey was often eaten from or with the comb, but sometimes it was just honey on its own so that the honey needed to be separated or extracted from the comb. Think of all these steps! But then again, think of the reward of that delicious, rich, and very sweet honey! Now think of how and why honey is compared to My word. Honey was the sweetest thing available to them in those days. Gold was the most valuable. So for My word to explain the sweetness and value of its knowledge is quite important. Consider all the steps above for actually obtaining the honey. Now think of My word. Take the steps to learn from My word, memorize it, study it, believe it, receive its truth into your innermost parts. Consider My precepts, laws and commandments and know how valuable and sweet they are to your life and soul! My Sweet Honey girl! How valuable you are to Me! I gave you that beautiful Word and I gave you my only Immaculate Son to be your Savior!

Immense love from,

The Only Wise God

> How sweet are Your words to my taste—sweeter than honey in my mouth! Psalm 119:103 BSB

> The precepts of the LORD are right, giving joy to the heart. The commands of the LORD are radiant, giving light to the eyes. The fear of the LORD is pure, enduring forever. The decrees of the LORD are firm, and all of them are righteous. They are more precious than gold, than much pure gold; they are sweeter than honey, than honey from the honeycomb. By them your servant is warned; in keeping them there is great reward. Psalms 19:8-11 NLT

By the time this child is old enough to choose what is right and reject what is wrong, he will be eating yogurt and honey. Isaiah 7:15 NLT (prophecy about Jesus)

Eat honey, my son, for it is good; honey from the comb is sweet to your taste. Proverbs 24:13 NLT

DEAR REJOICING GIRL,

Rejoice in Me always. I will say it again: Rejoice! To rejoice means to feel or show great joy or delight. Do you feel great joy and delight when you think of Me My girl? Why not? Is it fear that holds you back? Are you not sure how I feel about you? Or maybe you think I am just waiting for you to mess up and then I will happily punish you. Do you really know Me, Me child? Do you honestly know My character or how much I love you? If you did, I don't think rejoicing would be a problem! I don't think anyone could hold you back from leaping with joy and exultation! So what is holding you back from truly learning about Me, searching Me and My character out in My word? The God and Maker of the entire universe loves you! Sent His Son to die for you. Wants a relationship with you! In Greek, the word rejoice means, be glad- to delight in God's grace. The root for both the words joy and grace are the same. Therefore, they have the same core meaning. When was the last time you delighted in or rejoiced in Me or My grace? Oh My girl! You are missing out on so much if you cannot revel in Me, My character, My grace or how much I love you! Take the blinders off your eyes and do not let the evil one fool you anymore! Take joy, delight, pleasure, exhilaration, and gladness in the grace and love I offer you My child! Take joy in your God and King! I will say it again: Rejoice!

So much love from your,

Joy Giver, The God of Grace.

Rejoice in the Lord always. I will say it again: Rejoice! Phil. 4:4 NIV

You make known to me the path of life; you will fill me with joy in your presence, with eternal pleasures at your right hand. Psalm 16:11 NIV

But may the righteous be glad and rejoice before God; may they be happy and joyful. Psalm 68:3 NIV

DEAR IMAGINATIVE GIRL,

You cannot even imagine what I have in store for you when you get to heaven! But I want you to try! Thinking about what a reward heaven will be will help you get through some of these challenges on earth. My word says that no eye has seen, nor ear has heard, nor entered into your heart and imagination what I have in store for you! (1 Corinthians 2:9) It will be way above the natural beauty that you can imagine, way beyond the most amazing music you have ever heard and the light, oh the light will be gorgeous! When you think about a stunning place that you have been to or seen, some kind of natural beauty, when you remember it later, doesn't it feel peaceful and calm? Ok, again, what you will feel, hear, see, smell, taste and touch will be incredible and SO very much more...So why am I telling you this today? It's about: HOPE. If you have hope of heaven and being with Me and My Son, and seeing all I have prepared for you; it will give you great hope. If you asked My Jesus into your heart and told others about that, you not only have that hope, but you have assurance of heaven! I want you to have that hope and assurance. I want you to be looking forward to heaven. I want it to spur you on to doing this life, in My will and way, helping you to remember that heaven will be worth it all! Use your very limited human imagination, and try to think about what I have in store for you is so much more... You will be awed...Fight the good faith, Finish the race, Be strong, Have hope!

An incredible agape love from your,

Genius Creator: Maker of heaven and earth, and your Father God

That is what the Scriptures mean when they say, "No eye has seen, no ear has heard, and no mind has imagined what God has prepared for those who love him." 1 Corinthians 2:9 NLT

You alone are the LORD. You made the heavens, even the highest heavens, and all their starry host, the earth and all that is on it, the seas and all that is in them. You give life to everything, and the multitudes of heaven worship you. Nehemiah 9:6 NIV

Now unto him who is able to do immeasurably more than all we ask or imagine, according to his power that is at work within us, to him be glory in the church and in Christ Jesus throughout all generations, for ever and ever! Amen. Ephesians 3:20–21 NIV

DEAR COURAGEOUS GIRL,

So do not fear for I am with you… I could stop right there My girl because the very fact that I am with you, (and be assured, I am always with you), is enough to keep you from fear. Do not be dismayed, disheartened, distressed, depressed or deprived of courage… for I am your God. Let's pause again here. Do you see the beauty, the incredible fact that The very God of heaven and earth is yours? Yours! I am yours and you are mine! Oh My daughter, can you fathom the magnificence of that statement alone? If that is all I said to you today, that statement: I am yours and you are mine, and you understood it and believed it with all your heart, you would be a changed person! Your heart could not contain the love and your courage, in light of it would be immense! I will strengthen you and help you. You are not on your own! You do not have to do things in your own strength. Ask Me for strength. Ask Me for help. I am waiting to hear from you and to help you. I will uphold you with my righteous right hand. I am holding you, supporting you, with you…So, let's go over the verse again in its entirety:

So do not fear, for I am with you; do not be dismayed, for I am your God. I will strengthen you and help you; I will uphold you with my righteous right hand. Isaiah 41:10 (NIV)

Remember these words my courageous girl: I am always with you and your strength comes from Me. So much love for you My girl,

From,

Your Righteous God

Have I not commanded you? Be strong and courageous. Do not be afraid; do not be discouraged, for the LORD your God will be with you wherever you go." Joshua 1:9 NIV

So be strong and courageous! Do not be afraid and do not panic before them. For the LORD your God will personally go ahead of you. He will neither fail you nor abandon you." Deuteronomy 31:6 NLT

For God has not given us a spirit of fear and timidity, but of power, love, and self-discipline. 2 Timothy 1:7 NLT

So be strong and courageous, all you who put your hope in the LORD! Psalm 31:24 NLT

DEAR PREPARED GIRL,

Are you ready? Are you expecting what is to come? Do not be afraid, I have rescued you to belong to me. I have called you by name, so now you are mine. When you go through the deep water, I will be with you. When you cross dangerous rivers, you will not drown. When you walk through fire, It will not burn you. The flames will not destroy you... I am not suggesting in the slightest that you do any of these things on purpose and then say: rescue me God! No! My purpose is to remind you that you will have trouble in this world. It's when! Not if! But there is a remedy My girl! My Son said,

"I have told you these things, so that in me you may have peace. In this world you will have trouble. But take heart! I have overcome the world." (John 16:33 NIV)

So I am telling you this and he has told you this in My word, so that you will be prepared, and that you will have peace with Me in the midst of it. There is nothing that surprises Me. I know the beginning of everything and I know the ending. And I especially know that you are My child and I hold you in My hand. No one can snatch you away from Me! So prepare your heart and mind with My word. And always remember that My Son is coming to get you soon and very soon My girl! Be expecting him and be a very prepared girl!

Love, from your,

All-Knowing Father

I give them eternal life, and they will never perish, and no one will snatch them out of my hand. My Father, who has given them to me, is greater than all, and no one is able to snatch them out of the Father's hand. John 10:28-29 ESV

"I have told you these things, so that in me you may have peace. In this world you will have trouble. But take heart! I have overcome the world." John 16:33 NIV

Do not be afraid, I have rescued you to belong to Me. I have called you by name, so now you are mine. When you go through deep waters, I will be with you. When you cross dangerous rivers, you will not drown. When you walk through fire, it will not burn you. The flames will not destroy you... Isaiah 43:1b-3a NLT

DEAR OBEDIENT GIRL,

The words obey, obedience and obedient are not words that are used much in your modern world today. Not unless they are referring to how an animal behaves or does not behave. But the words and their meanings are not something that will ever become obsolete to Me. Nor should they to you. They are extremely important words to Me, something I expect and therefore words and actions that you should highly esteem. Obedient means: obeying or willing to obey; complying with or submissive to authority. I am your ultimate authority. I am your God, King, Master, and Maker. I deserve your greatest respect and obedience. If you love Me and know, really know how much I love you and want the best for you, you will want to obey. I always have your best interest at heart, I know and can see the entire picture and scope of your life and I know the plans that I have for you. They are good plans. Submitting to and obeying Me is not the same as submitting to human authority. I'm sure many humans have let you down or given you a bad example of an abuse of power. Maybe it was a parent, a teacher, someone in the church or someone else who should have been protecting you in some sort of authoritative position. Let's just recognize that now. Someone, maybe multiple people have let you down. How they have treated you was completely wrong, and doing what they told you to do or trusting that they had your best interest at heart was almost impossible. So you want to throw the word out... I am sorry My girl for their actions and how it hurt you. It was their job to look out for you, protect you, love you and teach you. Their mistreatment of you has caused you to be very wary of anyone in authority over you... But there are legitimately those that you should respect, listen to and even obey. My word says that you must and it has no flaw. The evil one and humans have completely messed up the chain of protection and authority and how they were designed to work. Do search out in my word what your role is to be in this area and do it. That's what it boils down to. I am your ultimate authority and the entire universe is under my jurisdiction. If I say something, you can trust it. If I say not to do something, you can completely trust that also. Remember, what I ask of you in My word is from a God with complete wisdom and love for you. I know what is best for you My obedient girl and I love you so much! Trust Me and Listen and obey...

So much love from your,

Ultimate Authority, Master and Maker of the entire universe.

> I will hasten and not delay to obey your commands. Psalms 119:60 NIV

> But don't just listen to God's word. You must do what it says. Otherwise, you are only fooling yourselves. James 1:22 NLT

> Jesus replied, "Anyone who loves me will obey my teaching. My Father will love them, and we will come to them and make our home with them. John 14:23 NIV

DEAR FRUITFUL GIRL,

It is My desire to see fruit in your life. Are you fruitful My daughter? Is your life characterized by love, joy, peace, patience, kindness, goodness, faithfulness, gentleness, and self-control? Or is it characterized by hate, despair, fear, impatience, rudeness, evilness, being unreliable, abrasiveness, harshness and undisciplined? The one way is the way of My Spirit and it is very fruitful. The other way is living by the flesh and it brings much unhappiness for you and anyone else in your life! The way of the Spirit is life and health and peace and the way of the flesh is death. There's only one way that is right and beautiful. A fruitful life is a life that bears fruit. It is living with my fruit, growing each day and actually producing this fruit. It's not a chore or a burden but the most peaceful and beautiful way you can live. It is peaceful and happy and not only will you enjoy that life but those who work with you, your family, and those that come into contact with you will all be blessed by this Spiritual fruit in your life. You can only be fruitful if you are connected to The Vine. Remain in Me and I will remain in you. To remain means to live, dwell, abide. I am your strength, your supply, your life Giver. With Me you can do anything and without me you can do nothing. Stay connected to Me, your Vine: Read My Word, spend time with Me, pray much and often, and you will grow and produce much fruit! I Love you My fruitful girl!

So much love from,

The Vine.

I am the Vine; you are the branches. If you remain in me and I in you, you will bear much fruit; apart from me you can do nothing. John 15:5 NIV

But the Holy Spirit produces this kind of fruit in our lives: love, joy, peace, patience, kindness, goodness, faithfulness, gentleness, and self-control. There is no law against these things! Galatians 5:22–23 NLT

So as to walk in a manner worthy of the Lord, fully pleasing to him, bearing fruit in every good work and increasing in the knowledge of God. Colossians 1:10 ESV

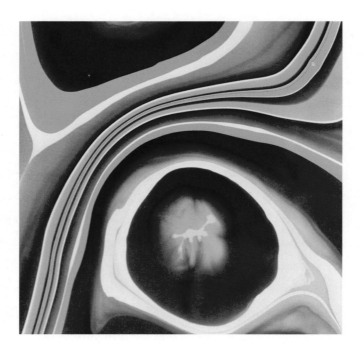

DEAR HUMBLE GIRL,

My dear humble daughter. I know you've heard this your whole life, but I'd like for you to listen and consider again with eyes and ears and mind wide-open. You've lost the awe and wonder of this beautiful story...... The very Son of God came to earth as a totally helpless babe, to the poorest of the poor. They were staying in a stable and they placed My precious Jesus, wrapped in rags, into an animal's feeding trough. Jesus, the very powerful Son of God, left exquisite heaven with all it's glory and light and beauty and peace and love... Consider this... For the mind of a helpless babe with no power, to this world with all its problems... Why? Simple. Because•of•Love. He did it for the love of his children. It is the most profound and humble act anyone has ever accomplished. Sometimes, when you are too familiar with something, you lose the amazement and awe. But I sent My son, My only son, for you My daughter, his precious and sinless life to pay the ransom for your sins so that you would be forgiven and free and so that you could be with Me for all eternity. So why did I entitle this letter; Dear Humble Girl? Because My child, I am calling you to be humble. Everything you have, every gift or blessing, absolutely everything is a gift from Me. Is there anything there to brag about if everything you have and are is from Me? Do you have talents, wisdom, knowledge, expertise, kindness, and service? Have you used these talents, etc. and grown more skilled or wise with them? Wonderful. They were and are gifts from Me. So live your life for My honor and glory child. This is what

I require of you and to do what is right, to love mercy, and to walk humbly with your God.

So much love from your,

High and holy God and loving and tender Father.

> He has shown you, O man, what is good; And what does the LORD require of you But to do justly, To love mercy, And to walk humbly with your God? Micah 6:8 NKJV

> My hands have made both heaven and earth; they and everything in them are mine. I the Lord have spoken! I will bless those who have humble and contrite hearts, who tremble at my word. Isaiah 66:2 NIV

> Humble yourselves before the Lord, and he will exalt you. James 4:10 ESV

DEAR ADORING GIRL,

Everyone needs something to worship and adore. They search high and low to find something they love, and then put their money, energy and distraction into it. Unfortunately their search and efforts are useless if they are not pouring those efforts into Me. You see, what they need, what you need, is to adore Me! Maybe you don't even think of this as a 'need' but it is My girl. You were actually made for this! Let's talk about what the word actually means; it means to honor and worship with a profound reverence. To love in the highest degree. To regard with the utmost esteem, love and respect. Awe. Adore as with bended knee. That's much more than you realized it meant, right? You thought it was casual like, I adore this, I love that... But it is SO much more as it pertains to your LORD, God, Savior and King. Think of everything you have pursued in your life... Love, family, education, fame, money, food, clothing, things, a special group or team to be connected to... Do they ever satisfy for more than a moment? If they did, why would you continually want more or something different to pursue again and again? The need to adore is real. Maybe you would never have put it into those terms, that what you needed to do for satisfaction was to adore. But basically that's what it is and your adoration will never, ever be satisfied when what you are chasing is any 'thing'. What you need, truly need is to adore and worship your God and King! I made you with this need and absolutely nothing else will satisfy you. Nothing else will bring you joy and fill you up. That is always My way daughter. When you give Me what you should: respect, adoration, worship, time, obedience, money, honor... I always give back to you and SO much more! Love, peace, joy, contentment, fulfillment... So my daughter, I am calling you and all my other children to; Oh come, let us worship and bow down: let us kneel before the Lord God, our maker. For he is our God; and we are the people of his pasture, and the sheep of his hand... (Psalm 95:6-7) I love you so, My beautiful worshiping daughter!

From your,

Loving, everlasting Father

> Yours, O LORD, is the greatness, the power, the glory, the victory, and the majesty. Everything in the heavens and on earth is yours, O LORD, and this is your kingdom. We adore you as the one who is over all things. 1 Chronicles 29:11 NLT

> God is Spirit, and His worshipers must worship Him in spirit and in truth." John 4:24 BSB

> Yours, O' LORD, is the greatness and the power, the glory, the victory, and the majesty. Everything in the heavens and on earth is yours, O' LORD, and this is your Kingdom. We adore you as the one who is over all things. 1 Chronicles 29:11 NLT

DEAR NEW GIRL,

My daughter! I can make all things new and you are a new creation! All your yesterdays and regrets and shame are in the past. Listen carefully, I am about to do a new thing, now it will spring forth; will you not be aware of it? I will even put a road in the wilderness, rivers in the desert. (Isaiah 43:19 AMP) So when you think there is no way forward and there is not a road for you to walk upon, I will show you – "This is the way, walk in it." (Is. 39:21 NIV) I will lead you. I will guide you. I will strengthen you. But My girl, you will have to listen and follow to be on that new road. You will have to let go of the baggage of the past. Drop it!

It is not serving you.

It is not helping you.

It is not blessing you.

It is not giving you joy.

It is not giving you peace.

It is not strengthening you.

It is not calming your fears.

It is not giving you hope.

It is not giving you a future.

It is not loving you.

It is not encouraging you.

It is not giving you justice.

It is not giving you grace.

It is not giving you redemption or forgiveness.

It is not giving you purpose.

It is not giving you mercy.

It's not giving you victory or wisdom.

It is not giving you life!

And it, this past you are so desperately hanging onto, is certainly not giving you freedom! No, no, no My girl! A million times over- No! The wrongs that others have done to you, the repeated remembrances of the past, and the places that you have sinned are baggage and useless to you! Let go! Only I can offer you all those beautiful things above! And I DO My girl! Let go My daughter and walk in My hope and future. You are a new creation and you are My new girl!

From,

Your Father,
Who makes all things new!

> He who is seated on the throne said, "I am making everything new!" Then he said, "Write this down, for the words are trustworthy and true." Revelation 21:15 NIV

> Because of the Lords great love we are not consumed, for his compassions never fail. They are new every morning; great is your faithfulness. Lamentations 3:22-23 NIV

DEAR PROMISE GIRL,

You are My daughter of promise and such a promising girl! I mean that in the most positive sense. As in promising, I don't mean, Oh, maybe she'll be good enough someday... or she shows promise... No, what I mean is that I have so many promises in My bible and you believe them! The "promising" is about you accepting them personally for yourself and living with the belief and knowledge of what I have promised. All the wonderful promises and hope for this world and the very great promise for your eternity with Me in heaven. So what are my promises for you My child? Do you know them by heart?

- I love you with an everlasting love.
- Through belief in My Son, you have everlasting life.

- I hear you when you pray.

- I will never leave you nor forsake you.

- I will work everything out for your good.

- I have plans to prosper you and not to harm you, to give you hope and a future.

- Through Christ, I have given you everything you need to live a godly life.

- My mercies are new every morning!

- Christ has gone to prepare a place for you in heaven. In My house are many mansions.

And there are SO many more My girl! Search them out for yourself in My word. They will be treasures to you!

So much agape love from,

Your Father Who has given you such great and precious promises! And I never go back on my word!

> Because we have these promises, dear friends, let us cleanse ourselves from everything that can defile our body or spirit. And let us work toward complete holiness because we fear God. 2 Corinthians 7:1 NIV

> Let us hold tightly without wavering to the hope we affirm, for God can be trusted to keep his promise. Hebrews 10:23 NIV

DEAR STORMY GIRL,

You have weathered many storms in your life! Emotional storms, storms of sickness, marital storms, storms of loss… Loss of loved ones, loss of life as you knew it, financial storms, storms of abuse, and storms with your children… Some of those things you handled well, some not so much. All of them were things you would not have chosen to go through. Maybe your attitude is stormy right now. Are you mad at me My daughter for allowing you to go through so much? Do you trust Me? No, really, be honest. I already know the answer. Do•you•trust•Me? That's what it boils down to. Do you trust that there is a reason for the storms? Do you trust that I will use these things to grow your character and strength? Do you trust that I will redeem all this you have been through? Possibly, the redemption may happen in this earthly life and perhaps not until your eternal life… And one more very important thing, do you believe that I was and I am with you in the storms and brought you through them? I will never leave you nor for sake you. I am with you every step of the way, in every stormy gale, in the wind and in the waves, in the ice and snow, and the dry heat of desert, I am there. Always, I am there… Trust Me My girl. I am your foundation, your Rock and anchor, and also your peace! Hold onto Me! Believe in My promises for your future. Just keep trying to do the right thing, the next thing… And pray, pray, pray. Ask Me to make a way for you through this, and to still the wind and the waves. Remember that I am in control of the timing and I always have a loving reason for it. My dark and stormy girl, the light of dawn is coming, the new day arrives and with that, beautiful hope for your future. Hang on My strong girl, weeping may last through the night but joy comes in the morning. When you see that light coming, My light, you will be the light filled girl, filled with hope and the storms will be behind you. (But I must be true to My character and be honest- The storms may cease,at least for a time My girl...). In the meantime, know that you can always trust Me and I am here for your struggles, fears and tears. I will bring you through...

So much love from,

The Maker of the wind and the waves, but also, He Who calms them. And your Rock and the anchor of your soul.

He got up, rebuked the wind and said to the waves, "Quiet! Be still!" Then the wind died down and it was completely calm. Mark 4:39 NIV

God has said: "Never will I leave you, never will I forsake you. Hebrews 13:5b BSB

For he commanded and raised the stormy wind, which lifted up the waves of the sea. Psalm 107:25 NIV

He stilled the storm to a whisper; the waves of the sea were hushed. Psalm 107:29 NIV

Be merciful to me, O God, be merciful to me, for in you my soul takes refuge; in the shadow of your wings I will take refuge, till the storms of destruction pass by. Psalm 57:1 NIV

Trust in the LORD with all your heart; do not depend on your own understanding. Seek his will in all you do, and he will show you which path to take. Proverbs 3:5-6 NLT

DEAR FOLLOWING GIRL,

My girl, are you a follower or a leader? They are both good and necessary actually, depending on who you are following. It is Me you must follow, the LORD your God, and you must revere Me. Keep My commands and obey Me. Serve Me and hold fast to Me. (Deuteronomy 13:4 NIV)

- Follow Me
- Follow My way and direction
- Follow My Son
- Follow My Word
- Follow My Holy Spirit's prompting and leading

My Son said, "If anyone would come after me, let him deny himself and take up his cross daily and follow me. (Luke 9:23 NAS)

Following Me allows you to walk in the light. When you are doing all of this, you make a great leader and others can follow you. Remember that you are My ambassador and others will notice you as My luminary. So make sure that you continue to follow all My ways, so if others follow how you behave, I will still be honored. Stay strong until the end dear girl! I love you My precious following and leading girl!

So much love from,

The LORD your God

Teach me, LORD, the way of your decrees, that I may follow it to the end. Psalms 119:33 NIV

Seek his will in all you do, and he will show you which path to take. Proverbs 3:6 NIV

When Jesus spoke again to the people, he said, "I am the light of the world. Whoever follows me will never walk in darkness, but will have the light of life". John 8:12 NIV

DEAR LIGHT-FILLED GIRL,

You are called to look to the Light, be filled with the Light, reflect the Light and use the light as a lamp. That's a lot of light and a very bright life and existence. Your eye is the lamp of your body. When your eyes are healthy, your whole body is full of light. (Matthew 6:22 NIV) What are your eyes seeing My girl? My Word, or the world? For my word is a lamp to your feet and a light for your path. (Psalm 119:105 NIV) When I say that you're called to look to the light, that light is Jesus! In Him is life and that life was the light of all mankind. His light shines in the darkness, and the darkness can never extinguish it. (John 1:4 NIV) And Jesus said, "I am the light of the world, he who follows me will not walk in the darkness, but will have the light of life." John 8:12 (NIV)

Love,

The Light of the World

> You, LORD, keep my lamp burning; my God turns my darkness into light. Psalm 18:28 NIV

> In the same way, let your light shine before others, that they may see your good deeds and glorify your Father in heaven. Matthew 5:16 NIV

> The LORD is my light and my salvation – whom shall I fear? The LORD is the stronghold of my life – of whom shall I be afraid? Psalm 27:1 NIV

And whatever you do, whether in word or deed, do it all in the name of the Lord Jesus, giving thanks to God the Father through him. Colossians 3:17 NIV